THE DAN BONGINO SHOW SURVIVAL GUIDE

THE DAN BONGINO SHOW SURVIVAL GUIDE

CRAZY STORIES, HIDDEN MESSAGES, AND GOLDEN RULES

JIM VERDI PRODUCER OF THE DAN BONGINO RADIO SHOW

Liberatio
Protocol

A LIBERATIO PROTOCOL BOOK
An Imprint of Post Hill Press
ISBN: 979-8-88845-368-1
ISBN (eBook): 979-8-88845-369-8

The Dan Bongino Show Survival Guide:
Crazy Stories, Hidden Messages, and Golden Rules
© 2024 by Jim Verdi
All Rights Reserved

Cover Design by Cody Corcoran

Post Hill Press
New York • Nashville
posthillpress.com

Published in the United States of America
1 2 3 4 5 6 7 8 9 10

For my amazing wife, Toni. You have been my purpose, my reason for wanting to be better, and the only person I've ever wanted to be on this journey with. Love you.

Contents

INTRODUCTION

Communication is the most basic function that a society must have to be able to be successful. Going back to the hunter-gatherers, developing a certain common language was necessary to survive. Men had to have ways to develop plans for the hunt, especially when they had to take down animals much larger than they were. They also found it necessary to record their exploits on the walls of caves showing us what these plans looked like. When we look back at more modern man, yet still in ancient civilizations, man was able to communicate complex ideas to develop things like the pyramids and other wonders of the world. Stories were always a part of their communication process. In Ancient Greece, stories like *The Iliad* were recounted by mouth over and over again until eventually they were committed to the written word. Great orators were revered throughout history because the spoken word and the ability to clearly communicate stories to others were crucial to the development of societies and cultures. From Pericles to Cicero to Patrick Henry to Frederick Douglass to Winston Churchill to Martin Luther King Jr., history is filled with men we deem as great because of the way they were able to speak and write. We remember their ideas. We as a people need to have that line of communication to feel connected to others, and we are constantly developing more and more ways to do that; the latest and greatest example is the rise of social media. But the spoken word truly holds a special place in the pantheon of human history because, if done by the right person and done correctly, it can grab hold of your heart, soul, and mind and bring you close to that person, influencing your very thoughts and feelings. The ability to speak well is a very powerful tool to have in your arsenal. That's why radio has played such an integral role in the historic events of the twentieth century and still does today.

While many in *The Dan Bongino Show* audience can point to the rise of Rush Limbaugh as the beginning of their talk radio experience, the format itself dates back to the 1920s, albeit in a very primitive form. As we'll discuss in this book, of course, government interference regulated the taking of phone calls and broadcasting them, so much so, that many stations would never even approach doing such a thing for fear of massive fines or jail—all this in the name of "protecting" innocent people. So much for freedom of speech. It wasn't until the 1940s that the talk radio format you're familiar with began to take shape. A man named Joe Pyne could arguably be credited as being the first political talk show host. A radio nomad (he kept getting fired for injecting his personal opinions into his stint as a local DJ), he finally found his home in Atlantic City, New Jersey, where he honed his show idea about expressing his opinions and ideas on WFPG. Satisfied with what he had created, he eventually wound up at WILM in Delaware, a place he had previously worked, and in 1951 debuted his show, *It's Your Nickel*, the cost of a phone call then, in which he would take calls and argue with the callers. Although the Fairness Doctrine, which stated that both points of view of a political issue must be represented on the radio, had existed since 1949, Pyne did his show the way he wanted anyway, giving his opinions, arguing with callers, and insulting anyone he didn't agree with. His show became so big, he eventually moved out to Los Angeles where he was on KABC, a station we are currently broadcasting *The Dan Bongino Show* on. Pyne eventually went on to do TV, and because he was a heavy smoker, got lung cancer and tragically died at the age of forty-five.

But the Fairness Doctrine of 1949 would have a major impact on all of radio and television. It was originally put into place because, according to the Reagan Library, "Lawmakers became concerned that the monopoly audience control of the three main networks, NBC, ABC and CBS, could misuse their broadcast licenses to set a biased public agenda." As much of an abomination as the Fairness Doctrine was in squelching free speech, they seemed to be prescient in their fears, as we see those very networks demonstrating their biases today. So, from the 1950s to the 1970s, the Fairness Doctrine was used as a threat to radio stations looking for license renewal. You will abide, or you will lose your license. But in 1981, something happened that would put the Fairness Doctrine in peril: the swearing in of Ronald Reagan as president of the United States.

Reagan appointed a communications attorney who served on his campaign staff in 1976 and 1980 as chairman of the FCC. Mark Fowler proceeded to dismantle the Fairness Doctrine under the pretense that it was a First Amendment violation. The year 1987 saw a new FCC chairman, Dennis Patrick, who put together a panel that eventually repealed it altogether. There were fears about this from the Reagan administration because the press was already lambasting anything President Reagan was doing, and removing the Fairness Doctrine, in their minds, would make things worse. But they did not have the foresight to see what was on the horizon.

Rush Hudson Limbaugh III was born into a family steeped in the legal profession. His grandfather, father, and brother were lawyers, his uncle a federal judge. This was supposed to be the path he would follow. But Rush had other ideas. He fell in love with radio at the age of sixteen, getting his first job at that age at KGMO. He would go on to other radio jobs and got fired from several. That is not unusual in radio; as a matter of fact, it's kind of expected. If you haven't been let go from a radio job, you're one of the rare few. Rush then went on to work for the Kansas City Royals as director of group sales and special events, but his passion for radio never wavered. He went back to Kansas City and, for the first time, used his real name in hosting a radio show that again he got fired from. But that landed him his big break. He did a talk show in 1985 at KFBK in Sacramento and built a strong enough following that eventually when the Fairness Doctrine was repealed in

1987, ABC Radio Networks executive Ed McLaughlin offered Rush a nationally syndicated radio show. Limbaugh accepted and moved to New York City to begin his noon to 2 p.m. show on WABC in New York and was initially broadcast on fifty-six stations across the country in 1988. These were AM radio stations that were an afterthought at the time, as FM radio programming was considered the Cadillac of radio broadcasting with its clear, crisp signal. AM was considered old and over, as it had a very deep bass mono sound that was outdated. But the AM band that no one could figure out how to make relevant again was about to experience a revival because of Rush Limbaugh. He was the right man at the right time and arguably can be credited with being the man who saved the AM band. He was also the man who would create the talk radio world that we know today. With the Fairness Doctrine out of the way, the constraints were off opinion talk radio. Whereas the major mainstream media were able to espouse their liberal views, hiding them in plain sight under the guise of "objective news," Rush tore the blinders off and exposed them for what they were. As he used to say, "I am equal time." Dan Henninger of the *Wall Street Journal* put it perfectly in his article, "Rush to Victory," in 2005 when he wrote, "The Fairness Doctrine was also an early nuclear option: If a local broadcaster's news operation made the local congressman or his party look bad, Washington could threaten to blow up his broadcast license. Ronald Reagan tore down this wall in 1987 (maybe as spring training for

Berlin) and Rush Limbaugh was the first man to proclaim himself liberated from the East Germany of liberal media domination." For the three-plus decades that Limbaugh was on the air, he was talk radio. He set the standard. He became the voice of conservatism throughout the land, a yin to the mainstream media's yang, a thorn in the side of both liberal politicians, Presidents Clinton and Obama, and the many establishment Republicans who were more interested in appearing to look well at Washington, DC, cocktail parties than they were in doing what they were elected to do for their constituents. He inspired dozens of other hosts to take up the torch, and soon the AM band was filled practically 24/7 with conservative talk radio hosts. But Rush was always the king. He had our backs, and we had his, reaching as many as twenty-seven million Americans a week at some points. Until it all came crashing down.

CHAPTER 1

A FATEFUL DAY

February 17, 2021, is a life-changing date for so many involved in this story and for millions of people around the country and the world. It is the day Rush Limbaugh died.

I will never forget, as I was preparing another radio show I was producing at the time, hearing the devastating news. Kathryn Limbaugh, Rush's wife of ten years, announced his passing in the first segment of his radio show. With the familiar theme, The Pretenders' "My City Was Gone," fading into silence, Kathryn Limbaugh took to the microphone and welcomed the audience in, only to deliver the words none of us wanted to hear: "It is with profound sadness, I must share with you directly, that our beloved Rush, my wonderful husband, passed away this morning due to complications from lung cancer."

Boom. My heart sank at the news. I was devastated, as were millions of other Americans. I first heard Rush in 1990, when Jim Sharpe, a morning host I was producing at the time, told me about him. Tuning the dial to KGBS

1190 AM in Dallas and hearing him for the first time literally (I know Dan hates using that term, but in this case it's apropos) changed my life.

My dad, Jerry, was a navy guy, a conservative, and an early political influence in my life, even if I didn't even realize it. My mother, Andrea, was what you would imagine the perfect example of a mother to be in a 1950s TV show. We were what I guess you would refer to as lower middle class. Dad grew up a street kid after his father died unexpectedly when my dad was twelve years old. Rebellious and a lot of trouble, he saw he was heading for bad things and joined the navy to straighten his life out, which it did. My mom met my dad and became a young mom at nineteen. Life wasn't perfect, but I was molded by my parents' example of a strong nuclear family, what they talked about when it came to what was going on in the world, and by what I saw on the streets of Brooklyn, New York, in the 1970s. I grew up in the West Midwood-Kensington-Flatbush area of Brooklyn; St. Rose of Lima on Parkville Ave. was my rock. It's where I went to elementary school and served as an altar boy. Life on Newkirk Ave., where the school and church were, was almost idyllic. My best friend, Anthony Parisie (who still is to this day), lived down the street, and all the families were close and watched over all of us kids. But growing up in the city in the '70s was a challenge. When we moved to E. 7th St., I knew there was at least one family on our street that was "connected," if you know what I mean, and the local drug dealer lived about five houses down. But there never seemed to be any real trouble.

Luckily, I was able to experience another sort of life and again have my views molded by a particular area steeped in American tradition. My grandparents on my mother's side lived in Hampton, Virginia, a small town on the Chesapeake Bay. This is where my brother, Tom, and I (and much later, my sister, Kara) spent our summers and Christmases. There were no sidewalks on the streets in their neighborhood, just grass, small houses, and open fields. We would go down to the abandoned train trestle at the end of Old Pointe Road and go crabbing with my grandfather's crab traps. At dusk, we would sneak into the golf course on the other side of the trestle and go in the ponds to scoop up golf balls to sell later. Looking back on that, it never occurred to us how gross that water was, and we're lucky we didn't get some amoeba invading our brains. We would stay out all day long until it got dark, without a care in the world.

It was in this place that my love of history and the country really took hold. On Sundays, we would go to church at St. Mary Star of the Sea on Fort Monroe, the site of the famous first battle of the ironclads in the Civil War, the *Monitor* and the *Merrimack*. It was the place the Union held Jefferson Davis prisoner after the Civil War. There was a guard at a gate on the road leading into the fort. He would always salute as you drove on to the base. That was one of our favorite parts about going to the fort. We would always sit up higher in the back seat waiting to come up on the guardhouse for that salute. Of course, I would salute back. But my favorite part, and the part that really cemented in my head the greatness of America, was going to Williamsburg, Jamestown, and Yorktown every year. I always wanted to go whenever we went to Virginia. Walking the streets that Washington, Jefferson, Madison, Monroe, Thomas Paine, and so many of the other Virginians who crafted what was to become our nation walked, a nation that for the first time in human history finally posited that all men were created equal—that had a profound and everlasting impact on me.

So when I first heard the dulcet tones and that unique voice of Rush Limbaugh saying, "Greetings to you music lovers, thrill seekers, conversationalists all across the fruited plain. Time for another excursion into broadcast excellence hosted by me, America's real anchorman, Rush Limbaugh, with half my brain tied behind my back just to make it fair," and then espousing ideas and thoughts that I had always had but never heard expressed in a major medium, I was hooked.

If there was a major news event, you waited daily for Rush to come on and break it down. As so many of his listeners would, I would break down what I thought was going on with the situation in question, or an event that happened in the news, and then wait for Rush to address it to see if I was on the right track. When my thoughts tracked with his, it always brought a smile to my face. He was right; we were not mind-numbed robots. We were critically thinking people not willing to accept what we were being fed by the mainstream media anymore. He shined a light on what many of us never realized; we were being lied to daily by the people who were supposed to be holding the powerful to account. There was rarely a day that I did not listen to all three hours, and when the Rush Limbaugh app was developed, if I missed any of the show, I would go back and listen.

When he died, I knew my life would be different because I knew that keen analysis was going to be missing, especially in the current times post the Trump presidency, as we are all witnessing now. But I had no idea that other changes related to his passing would affect my life so tremendously—and the lives of Dan Bongino, Mike Sacco, and millions of Rush Limbaugh listeners.

CHAPTER 2

THE ROAD TO *THE DAN BONGINO SHOW*

I had given up on radio. Having worked in the industry since 1987, starting as a young intern at KLUV in Dallas, I had had enough. It wasn't the same anymore. I had always had a love for the medium. Growing up, Mom would have either WABC or Don Imus on WNBC on in the kitchen as I ate breakfast before school. As I grew older, I listened to 99X WXLO in New York and the great Jay Thomas, and in my teen years, WPLJ 95.5 FM New York's Best Rock was my jam. The great Pat St. John was an early influence, the voice of my summers. (Years later, we worked for the same company, which was a mind-blowing experience.) Then of course, there was baseball. I loved baseball, especially the New York Mets. The Mets at the time had Bob Murphy, Lindsey Nelson, and Ralph Kiner as their TV announcers, sharing announcing duties on the radio as well. There was just something magical about hearing a baseball game described on the radio: the way they painted the picture, relayed the drama playing out on the field, giving you information you didn't know you needed, but, dammit, you needed it. That is part of what made me fall in love with the game and my team. Of course, when I grew up, I was going to play center field for the Mets. Didn't quite work out though.

When I went to college, I wasn't sure what I wanted to do. As a kid, I always wanted to be an archaeologist, and that was my immediate thought. But in my mind, since I wasn't going to play baseball, I could do baseball play-by-play. So, I majored in communications. (I know, lame, but it worked out.) While in school, I started an unpaid internship with KLUV 98.7 doing "research" (it was a lot of bullshit that they never used), then they hired me as a part-time board op for a Saturday night satellite oldies show. I would call screen for the great Hubcap Carter sometimes during his lunchtime show, *The Blue Plate Special*, and call screen for others on the station from time to time. The news anchor at the time, Kate Garvin, and I became friends, and me wanting to get into sports, I asked if she ever got sound from any of the local teams. She said no, but if I wanted to do it, she'd get me the press credentials. And there I was off and running. I was in the press box for the Texas Rangers, on the sidelines for the Dallas Cowboys, and baseline on press row for the Dallas Mavericks. It was a dream come true. I was rubbing elbows with some of the great sports reporters of the DFW area. This was the start of my sportscasting career, or so I thought. After college, when the opportunity came for something full-time, I took whatever I could get for experience. Starting out in my first real full-time job as a morning show producer in 1989 at Star 105 in Dallas, an adult contemporary hits radio station, I was thrust into working with talents like Dana Carvey, Joe Piscopo, Jim Belushi, Leslie Nielsen, and more, as the station wanted to really highlight the "star" portion of their positioning. I had no idea what I was doing, but it was magical. But when the program director at the time who hired me, who was also the morning guy, was fired a month into my tenure for allegedly threatening to shoot Jim Belushi (at least that's the story I was told, but that's a story for another day), I knew my days were numbered. The GM, for whatever reason, did not like me. She didn't like me so bad that she had me pick up the new morning team she hired. I was to go pick them up at the airport and show them around. But apparently, she told them I was the guy she was going to fire. They felt pretty awkward, but I had no idea. Turns out they liked me and kept me on. But the format was doomed, and Westinghouse, who owned the station at the time, was selling the station. As in radio, when formats fail, layoffs happen—my first time getting fired. It was like a rite of passage. I was in the club now. The company that bought the station was brand new, what's commonly referred to in the industry as a "mom and pop," although this pop, John Hayes, had a lot of money and innovative ideas. He hired Rick Torcasso, who came up with the new concept for what this radio station was going to be. I was rehired months later by the country station that the 105.3 FM frequency had flipped to. Young Country was born. I didn't really want the job, but I was in a position where I had to take it. A kid from Brooklyn and country music? Are you kidding? I was hired to produce the morning show. It was the best job I ever had. I had a great program director in Dan Pearman. And I grew to love the music. In just three short years, we took that station from number thirty-two in the market to number three with number one in spitting distance. Then our tower fell down, and our backup was on the same tower. Our signal at that point couldn't penetrate a toaster. When CBS eventually bought the station, there was a pissing contest between Rick, the creator of the Young Country concept, and one of the execs at CBS. That executive proceeded to sabotage and destroy the format so he could chase his dream of building a "guy talk" radio station. I had been moved to producing and being the sidekick to the afternoon host, one of the funniest and most talented people I've ever worked with, AW Pantoja. Young Country would not die easy. We had a very passionate, loyal audience. But eventually, mostly due to the tragic tower collapse that claimed the lives of three people, the format lost out to the whims of the CBS executive.

The only people from Young Country to move to the talk station were me and AW. Neither of us had ever done talk radio before, but this was my baptism. It started out rough…really rough. But eventually, we found a groove and seemed to be heading in the right direction. But when the station had the opportunity to get Howard Stern in syndication, they had to let a show go. Guess who got the boot. That was fine with me though, because I didn't want to do that kind of talk anymore. It was not in my character, and I was uncomfortable with a lot of what we did. The saddest part is, I would never get to work with AW again. So, there I was, out of work, with a wife and three-year-old son, and a daughter on the way. And then my wife lost her job. We were in a desperate situation.

I had gotten into radio to be a sportscaster. Obviously, things took a different path. But ESPN was moving into DFW. I applied there and was certain with my experience I could land a pretty good job with them and start living my dream. Alas, what they had left was a morning board operator position with hourly *SportsCenter* reports. The pay was way less than I was making at Young Country. But I had to take it. We needed the money and the insurance. It was a fine job. I kept pushing for opportunities, but for whatever reason, the program director, Scott Masteller, had seen others better suited for his vision. I never held it against him and would never say a bad word about him. He was good to me in many ways, especially giving me another chance after leaving the station.

A year after starting at ESPN, my old GM at Young Country, Scott Savage, called and asked if I would be interested in a project he was starting. He and some partners were going to start a women's talk radio network (talk radio popped into my life for a third time). He offered me a good position, good pay, with a chance for advancement right away, and I took it. Many of the people from Young Country in promotions and sales, as well as Holly Stone (aka Katie Pruett) as program director and the amazingly talented Stubie Doak as production director, were there; it was like getting the band back together. We hired a great air staff, hit the air, got amazing press coverage. It was off to an incredible start. Three days on the air and Friday came. There was no money to pay us. The owner hadn't secured the loan that he told Scott and his partners that he had. The station was done. I called Scott Masteller back, and he said my position was already filled. But he hired me back anyway part-time, giving me as many hours as he could as well as other opportunities. I'll forever be grateful for that. (I would find out later that Dan actually had Scott as a program director when he was at WMAL as well.)

In 2004, I was offered a job at Radio Disney, reunited with my old program director from Young Country, Dan Pearman, and wrote and produced content for kids for the next ten years. It was a wonderful creative experience. But in 2014, The Walt Disney Company decided to move the operation to Burbank. They gave a ridiculous token offer for me to move out there, and of course, I couldn't accept. It was at this point I decided I'd had enough of radio and needed to look for something else to take me to retirement. This is when fate intervened again.

I was approached by an executive with Westwood One named Gary Reynolds about doing some vacation fill-in work producing a famous national talk show. Knowing the reputation of the host, He Who Should Not Be Named, I had to think about it. I knew that one of his former producers just a few weeks earlier went downstairs for a smoke and never went back up—just got in his car and left. But I thought I could fill in for a few days and handle it. I accepted the job knowing it was just going to be on a limited basis and only temporary. It was just what I thought it would be. But everything was fine. I was exploring new fields to work in, trying to figure out where my path would take me next, and then…the executive producer got fired. I was immediately filling in every day. It was just me and Robert Barowski, someone I had worked with at ESPN when he was just getting started in radio. It was great working with Rob again. He had come a long way. Westwood One offered me the job full-time. When they named their salary, I laughed. They asked what it would take, and I told them they would have to double it, and then they did. Now what was I going to do? They were desperate. I needed a full-time job. Having a wife and kids, I accepted, of course.

Working for He Who Should Not Be Named was the most challenging job I ever had in my life. There were many times I was ready to walk out and never go back. But I stayed—for seven years, until Westwood One finally parted ways with him. I was told there would be an opportunity for me with the company once the show ended. It materialized for Rob but not for me.

There I was, like nearly every other radio nomad, looking for work again. I told myself I was out for good this time. But of course, I needed to make a living. He Who Should Not Be Named was going to do a podcast, three a week. He asked me to produce it, and I told him yes, as long as I was not doing it full-time, and it wasn't up to me to provide the content. "Why would I do it?" would be a logical question. Let's face it, producing content for a podcast or a radio show is not the hardest job in the world. It's not like doing HVAC work in an attic in the middle of summer in Texas or for that matter, actually putting a new roof on a home! Roofers are some of the hardest workers on the planet. It's not installing floors in homes, which I have done, and my knees can tell you that's not easy. And it's definitely not as hard as being a soldier, let's say in Afghanistan, who went through way worse things than I could ever imagine—missing family for months or years, their birthdays, holidays, giving up so much for people they don't even know. My point is to say that what I went through is nothing in comparison to that. The most stressful part of doing a radio show is the clock. You have to account for getting things done the second they need to be; there's no room for error. Now, with a podcast, the clock wasn't a factor, so the most stressful part of the job was gone. Of course, for three months I did it, and as I should have expected, it got gradually worse. I had just gotten to the point where I told him I was going just to put the audio together, and I wanted no other contact. And my phone rang. It was a call that changed everything for the better.

CHAPTER 3

CONVINCING DAN

The Dan Bongino Show needs one key ingredient, and if you don't have it, it's not going to work. It would literally be impossible to make it work. That ingredient would be Dan Bongino. If you're reading this, you're most likely a listener to Dan's podcast or radio show or have watched him on Fox News, so you're pretty familiar with his story. For those who aren't, here's a recap:

Dan was born in New York, lived on Long Island, and in about the third grade, moved to Queens when his parents divorced. There he lived on top of a bar that his family owned, and this is where he learned how tough life could be in the city. When he got older, he joined the NYPD and was assigned to the worst precinct in New York. He had wanted to join the Marines, but fate intervened, and the NYPD came calling. After a short time on the force, Dan decided to join the Secret Service. He worked his way up successfully to eventually be on the President's detail. That President was Barack Obama. After a time, realizing he

15

did not support President Obama's policies, he decided he could no longer in good faith continue in his position. So, he resigned. Not retired, resigned—meaning no pension, no benefits, nothing. He then tried politics, deciding to run for Senate in Maryland. He lost. He was talked into running for a congressional seat in Maryland. He barely lost. He moved to Florida and ran one more time for Congress. He lost. Broke, with a wife and young child, he was now looking for what his next step would be.

During his runs for office, Dan had become a presence on some TV outlets and figured out he had a talent for being able to articulate his positions. Networks had him on as a guest. He was also invited to fill in on some national radio shows. By invited, I mean he called Sean Hannity's producer and asked if he could fill in for him when he was out. Amazingly, he said yes and had him guest host for him. Then he had the opportunity to fill in for Mark Levin. That never happens, by the way. If you don't think God has a hand in things, you're dead wrong. He had a show on the weekend at WMAL in Washington, DC. This was Dan's introduction to how to do a radio show. But it wasn't radio where he saw his greatest success.

While in Florida trying to figure out what he was going to do next, Dan read an article about podcasting being the future of broadcasting. He decided to throw his hat in the podcast ring, knowing nothing about how to do it. He used $10,000 that he really needed for other things to buy the equipment needed to create a podcast. He recruited Joe Armacost, whom he knew from WCBM in Baltimore, to help him. It was a slow go at first, Dan learning how to assemble the content and present it on the podcast, Joe working for free for the most part to help him get this thing going, but eventually, the podcast became bigger and bigger, until it reached the top of the podcast charts. (See Dan's book *The Gift of Failure* for a deeper dive on the story.) Having a highly successful podcast and a huge presence on Fox News, things were rolling pretty well for Dan. Then, the unthinkable happened. Rush Limbaugh died. This left a deep hole in the conservative movement and in the radio industry.

Westwood One was courting Dan, but this was before Dan had been diagnosed with Hodgkin's lymphoma. Dan continued his podcast, even through chemo treatments, and thankfully, the cancer had gone into remission. Dan was not interested in making the commitment to a daily three-hour radio show, but because of his own experience, and the death of Rush Limbaugh, he knew someone had to step up, and whoever took the job was going to face strong headwinds. How do you replace a legend? Not only a legend, but the greatest of all time. Growing up a New York Yankees fan, Dan described it as being the guy to replace Mickey Mantle. No matter how good you are, you're not going to be Mickey Mantle. Knowing the challenges and the headwinds he was going to face, Dan decided to take the job. This is no small point. It was a risk on two ends: Dan having to be the voice that replaced Rush and Westwood One, which owned many of the stations Rush was on, putting him on the air on those stations.

As noted earlier, if you're reading this, you are probably a fan of the podcast, radio show, or TV show and have probably heard a lot about Dan's story. Since you invest your time in listening to the podcast, the radio show, or both, I thought it would be good to show you how he prepares every day. At least this is the way it started.

In the beginning, Dan was up by 4 a.m. every day. He'd grab some coffee and start looking for what's in the news. He already has pieces for the show from the previous day (more on that in a minute), and he starts sending those out to Joe, Gui Cohen, who handles the video portion of Dan's podcast, me, and Mike. Dan has a notebook where he writes out how he wants to lay out that day's show. He'll take the elements he wants to use (i.e., headlines, parts of stories, videos, and so on) and make notes about what he wants to say about each. He'll also look for a theme that can run through the show. Once he's mapped out and outlined the show, he'll call me, I'll conference in Mike, and Dan will conference Gui in. We do a rundown and put the show in order. From there, Gui will put together all the elements in order, and that's what you see on the podcast on Rumble. Joe handles the audio podcast that you can hear on any of your favorite places to download podcasts. I take the same list and make two sheets for Dan: one for headlines, one for audio.

Dan used to record the podcast at about 8 a.m., then do his morning workout, have some breakfast, check on the latest news, and then come upstairs to the studio for the radio show. Now, he's changed his schedule. He starts sending the next day's show a few hours after the radio show so he doesn't have to get up at 4 a.m. anymore. We still did our call at 7 a.m. EST to do the rundown until September of 2023, when Dan decided just to do it after he sent the content the same day after the radio show so he doesn't have to wake up as early anymore (even though he does). Sometimes he'll send additional things in the morning. He'll do his workout and come up to the studio where we'll finalize any additional material added to the show and then he's set to livestream the podcast on Rumble at 11 a.m. EST. We'll go over any breaking news or new additions to the show before we go on, then the show starts at noon Eastern. During the show, a lot is happening. In the breaks, Dan is reading your messages on Facebook, which inspire different ideas or bring up different points. He's also looking at the latest news and planning the next day's show by finding headlines, reading stories, finding audio, and taking notes on all of it. While we use the same rundown for the podcast and the radio, the shows rarely track the same way. When the radio show is over, Dan has several business meetings, sends the material for the next day's show, does the rundown call, and then he's able to finally have family time.

If you're a longtime podcast listener, you've heard about Joe and Gui, but you may not know a lot about them. Gui Cohen is a talented young man. Born in Brazil, he came to America in 2013 to go to film school in Sarasota, Florida. After he graduated, he moved to New York City where he worked for the country's oldest pro-Israel organizations as a media strategist. This is where his political ideology began to take shape. He saw the absolute hatred and antisemitism harbored by those on the left, and it strengthened his conservative viewpoint and made him want to take action to fight harder against it. He was always into politics, but his passion for the Israeli situation was the catalyst for driving him towards conservatism. He loved the job, but New York wasn't his bag of donuts. Like many others, when COVID hit, he lost his job because no one wanted to do videos anymore. His wife, Kim, was working freelance, and the place she was working for was based in Miami, so they moved back to Florida. While in Florida, he saw an ad on Benny Johnson's Twitter account for an in-house video producer. He applied, got interviewed, and was hired. The job just happened to be doing a video version of Dan Bongino's podcast. Dan liked what he saw on Gui's reel and thought he was the right man for the job. So, in March of 2021, about the same time I was hired to produce Dan's radio show, Gui was hired to do the video portion of Dan's podcast.

Now if you're an avid podcast listener, you surely know Joe. Joe has probably the most interesting story of all of us. A native of Maryland, born in Baltimore, Joe started playing drums at the age of six. It seemed to come naturally to him. As he got older, he wanted his future to involve being a musician. He played in a lot of popular bands in the area, was voted best drummer in Baltimore, played in LA in the bands Mal & Val and Top Jimmy and the Rhythm Pigs, and in England, where he was asked to audition and was a finalist to be the drummer for Judas Priest! While he was having the time of his life, he just wasn't making any kind of money. So, he moved back to Baltimore and went to the Broadcasting Institute of Maryland and started working at WFBR in Baltimore as an intern, then went to WCBM and worked there for thirty years. He worked with the legendary Tom Marr and eventually made his way to the morning show, which he did for almost twenty years. That's where Joe met Dan. Joe thought Dan was a natural at being a radio host and even told Dan, "You could be the next Rush Limbaugh," but Dan scoffed at the notion. When Dan had looked into podcasting, he approached Joe, and they put a plan together and decided to start doing a podcast. Neither knew much about podcasts, but they'd venture on this journey to find out about them. There was no need for a radio station or anyone else to start a show. So, they started in his basement, and things were taking off. It took almost a week to get our first 100 listeners, which at the time was very good because 100 to 110 downloads of the song or of a show was about average with this budding new platform. Joe told Dan he was all in and wanted to take this ride with him no matter where it went but believing that it was going to go far. He worked for free for three years, doing his radio job and then going to do the podcast, and the rest is history.

CHAPTER 4

LET THERE BE LIGHT

Were it not for the seven years of working on that other show, all the rest of what is written here would never have happened. Kevin Delany of Westwood One called me in late February of 2021 and asked if I would be interested in producing the Dan Bongino radio show. I was familiar with Dan from his appearances on Fox News but really got to be familiar with his podcast while still working on the show with He Who Shall Not Be Named. Rob was working in the podcast division of Westwood One and at times was called to edit and post Dan's podcast. He would play it as he was editing, and to my ears, it was extremely compelling; Dan had a delivery that drew you in. You couldn't help but listen. It was like he grabbed you by the collar and was telling you something you had to hear as if your life depended on it. As we're seeing play out now, he's probably right. I knew he had a bout with cancer too, but in listening, you could never tell what he was going through. He was really good at weaving a story and always had receipts to back up what he was talking about. In my mind, he was the most logical person to step into the glaring void that Rush Limbaugh left. He had the talent, the delivery, the charisma you needed to do this. But he also had the balls to do it. Taking on the task of following the greatest talk show host ever was not for the meek, and meek is not among the descriptors for Dan Bongino anywhere you might find Dan Bongino descriptors. So when the opportunity came to be able to work with him, of course I said yes. Like Al Pacino in *The Godfather Part III*, every time I think I'm out, they drag me back in. If there was one job in radio I would take, it would be to produce the show that was going to air in the slot that I listened to religiously for three hours every day. I wanted to be a part of that as well. I knew I could help make this show great, and apparently, so did Westwood One. There was only one more person who needed convincing. That would be Dan Bongino. He didn't know me at all and wanted someone he knew to be the guy producing the show, and who could blame him. He had built something huge for himself, and it was his name on the line with the biggest spotlight being shone on him due to the legend he was replacing. I was a bit anxious about the call because I was told when they were discussing bringing me on with Dan, Paula was heard in the background saying, "He's a Mets fan," so I thought I had hills to climb at that point. So, we had a Zoom call with me, Dan, my boss Kevin, Theresa, and Bart Tessler, who was in charge of making this whole thing happen. Bart led the call, introduced us, and for the next hour, it was just me and Dan talking about everything: growing up in New York, the Mets and the Yankees, music, radio, just about everything. After an hour, I realized no one else had said a word except the two of us, and I asked if anyone else had anything to say. I think it was either Kevin or Bart who said, "We're just enjoying the show." It was evident we seemed to be a good fit. Dan gave the green light, and I was on board.

Once they had me, the next step was to go get Rob. Get the band back together! We had the chemistry, we could read each other's minds, we fed off of each other's creativity, and we both learned how to crank out top quality content under some of the most extreme and difficult circumstances in radio. But Rob had been working in the podcast division for a while now and also was working part-time at the Blaze and was really enjoying the ability to work from home. After many efforts to try and talk him into it, he declined. I asked him if he knew anyone who he thought would be a good fit for the job; he suggested Mike Sacco.

I talked with Mike on the phone first, and we had a lot in common. We both went to the same college, and we both loved baseball, among other things. But what sealed the deal for me was that he had national network production experience, as he had been one of the producers for Glenn Beck.

Mike had a Queens connection, as his mom was born there, and his dad was from Saddle Brook, New Jersey. He was born in Pittsburgh, Pennsylvania, and moved to Cleveland, Ohio, at two years old when the family had to move, as his dad had a new business opportunity with his uncle. Mike got interested in radio at a young age, spending time with his grandfather, who worked part-time delivering parts for the Ford Motor Company. Mike spent summers with him listening to the radio most of the day, every day. They would listen to Yankee games, jazz, and the news, but it was Mike's grandfather's favorite radio personality, Paul Harvey, who made a huge impression on him. This is what got him interested in talk radio from a very early age. He also learned about hard work and what it meant to put in sweat equity to get what you want. As a teenager, Mike worked at his father's shop washing floor mats until he saved enough money to buy his first car, a 1976 Chevy Camaro.

After his parents' divorce, Mike moved with his mom to Arlington, Texas, where he grew up. As a young adult, he tried sales for a while but hated it, however, he made enough money to take off for an extended period, travel, and he learned to flip houses. But radio seemed to be calling. A friend, Tommy Osbakeen, who at the time was imaging for Blair Garner's syndicated country show, *After Midnite*, later went on to work and image for the late great Kidd Kraddick's nationally syndicated morning show. Mike started to teach himself audio editing and picked up some work voicing and editing commercials, but 9/11 changed a lot for him. The demand for news/talk programming rose tremendously. His friend, Ian Miller, a thirty-year voice-over vet at CBS radio, called and told him about an opening for a board operator at legendary Dallas station KLIF. He called program director AnnMarie Petitto, and she told him if he could get there now, he could have the job. He was hired on the spot. Having never run a radio board before, AnnMarie gave him a twenty-minute tutorial on how to run a radio board, and that night he was the overnight board op from 12 a.m. to 6 a.m. After a few months running boards, he was offered a station producer job working with several of the local hosts, like Greg Knapp, Scott Anderson, and Darrell Ankarlo, eventually ending up producing for *Ankarlo Mornings*.

Mike spent five years at KLIF. After *Ankarlo Mornings*' contract didn't get renewed, and Cumulus bought out Susquehanna Radio, he was let go. But he made some good contacts, which led to him doing work with Fox News Radio, Glenn Beck, BBC1 Radio, and a bunch more at Clear Channel, Susquehanna, and iHeart stations. In 2009, his friend Kenny Newell asked if he would be interested in being an instructor at the American Broadcasting School. He took the job and was responsible for teaching a forty-three-week course that covered nearly every aspect of radio.

In 2015, Mike landed a job as a producer for Glenn Beck and Stu Burguiere, which he worked at until 2020. Out of work again (it's normal in this business, as you can see from both his experiences and mine), in March 2021, a posting went up for the Dan Bongino radio show. Westwood One needed two producers for the show. When Rob declined and gave me Mike's name, I talked with Mike over the phone. As I mentioned previously, I discovered we had a lot in common; both of us went to the University of Texas at Arlington, we both loved baseball, and Mike had worked for a national radio host, so I decided to meet in person. After a nice lunch and a good conversation, I gave the okay to my boss and he made the call. Once we got Mike on board, we were set to go. Now we just had to wait for launch.

CHAPTER 5

CREATING A SHOW FROM THIN AIR

One of the most satisfying things a creative person can do, actually, maybe the most satisfying thing is creating something from scratch, working on the blank canvas as they say. My radio career offered that to me a lot, and I relished every opportunity. At Star 105, we created that out of scratch, the same with Young Country, then the talk station that followed. Then I was able to help create a women's talk network from scratch, even though it did not end well. I was offered the chance to jump on with Radio Disney in 1996 to help create that, but I was on the number one show on the number three station in the market at that time, so I declined, only to wind up there eight years later and given the ability to use my creative juices to produce content that included voicing and writing characters that I had created for promos and commercials. Then there were the seven years in the desert where I had to come up with content every day and learn how to do it quickly. And then the opportunity came up to create a show for Dan.

In creating a radio show, you are constrained by the clock, first and foremost. There are start times, hard breaks, commercial breaks, and so forth. So you have to come up with the most entertaining and compelling material to surround the content Dan brings to the table.

One of my first goals was to come up with the show intro. That was a lot of pressure considering that at noon Eastern time each day, millions of people were used to hearing The Pretenders' "My City Was Gone" at that time. I had to try to pick something I thought would be ear-catching and fit Dan's personality. Dan had wanted to incorporate the song "Defy You" by The Offspring, but I needed more than that because at the front, when I hit the intro on the show, local stations are either promoting news coming up or running liners promoting either other shows or something else happening on the station. We have a production library I could (and did) use, and I had the song Dan wanted, but I needed that transitionary music to get us to the beginning of the show. I was having a really hard time figuring out what that would be and what would sound good enough to match the other two elements of the intro I already had. Then driving home from the studio one day, the song "Ready to Go" by Republica came on the radio. It's one of those songs that if you're driving, you better watch the speedometer, because it gets the adrenaline rushing. Like a lightning bolt it hit me. This was it! It was the perfect fit for the sound I was looking for.

Now I needed a voiced intro. Dan is a pretty humble guy, so he's not one to sing his own praises. Rush took care of his own intro, as "America's harmless, loveable little fuzzball, with three hours of broadcast excellence," and so on. So I had to come up with something to bring him in. The liner in the intro, read by amazing voice talent Pete Gustin, is completely different than what I had put together. I wrote something like, "Master of Media, Protector of Presidents," and Dan said, "Yeah, that's not really me." So we both came up with the current verbiage of: "From the NYPD to the Secret Service, to behind the microphone, taking the fight to the radical left and the putrid swamp...." Dan is the one who came up with "putrid swamp." He's very proud of that to this day.

Now that we had a show intro, we had to have bumpers (more on that later) and liners. I mentioned Pete Gustin earlier. He's a really amazing person. You've heard his voice on Fox News, on movie trailers, on video games, and more and may not have even known it. The amazing thing about him is he is blind, and this does not hinder his ability at all to deliver the liners I write. He also is a semiprofessional surfer! Not wanting to live life just comfortably, he was not going to let blindness deter him from living his best life. He took up surfing and inspired so many that he has a tremendous social media and video platform that reaches millions and shows people with disabilities that they don't have to just accept the status quo and can strive to do things others think you can't do.

So now that I had all the elements of a radio show, I had to figure out how to use them. I had everything recorded, and we had practice runs scheduled to test equipment and to figure out how to format it. This is like a puzzle, and you have to try to figure out where the pieces go. The week before we went live, we would do an hour of what the show would sound like. This is where we worked out the kinks before we were going to go live. I knew we were going to have bumpers coming out of every break, but how would we get back to content? Do I just go to Dan? What do I do with the four pages of liners I wrote and had Pete record? I decided the way the puzzle should work is bumper, liner, then Dan. I'm not one to tell Dan how to deliver his content. The way many hosts come into the show is giving the phone number and inviting calls. That's not Dan; he wants to get right to it. But I had to make sure the number was getting out there for listeners to at least process for whenever we would take calls. You can listen for this and notice if you haven't before, I do the phone number liner at the bottom of each hour. I know we only take calls in the last segment of the show, but it's important to get the phone number out there for people who would like to participate, and because radio audiences are forever tuning in and out, I like to make sure we hit as many people as we can with it. Just so you have it written down it's 844-484-3872. This was Kevin Delaney's brain child as it comes out to 844-4 THE USA.

So now we had the puzzle put together, and all we had to do is see how it was going to go. The week before we went live on the air, I don't think we even had everything worked out, but we were all comfortable enough for launch. We had only been doing the show for executives of Westwood One. Now it was time to go for real. The daunting task of filling the void created by the passing of a legend was upon us. I had DM'd James Golden, aka Bo Snerdley, saying I knew we could never replace Rush and that we were thinking of him on this momentous day. He responded thanking us for thinking of him and wishing us the best of luck. I was so thankful. Then on May 24, 2021, we went live.

CHAPTER 6

P1S—IF YOU KNOW, YOU KNOW

What is a P1? In radio terms, you have different categories of listeners: P1, P2, and P3. P3s are not even necessarily listeners; they are people who may have heard your station in the background at a restaurant, or waiting area, or somewhere else, but they are counted when it comes to ratings. P2s are people who tune you in some of the time but are not necessarily passionate about listening to you all the time. The P1 is the die hard. They are the most loyal listeners and the ones who make your radio show "can't miss" listening. These are the ones who pay the most attention to what is going on. We have developed many staples over the time we've been on the radio, and if you've been a listener for a long time, you might know what each of these are, but if you're a new P1 or want to be one, here is the list of our staples, not listed in any order except whatever comes to my mind first:

1. SWEET HOME ALABAMA—ODE TO DICK JOHNSON

Early in the life of the show, when Dan was standing up against the Cumulus vaccine mandate, certain "conservatives" chose to call him out after spending two weeks off the air in protest and saying Cumulus could have their mandate or have him but not both. Dan came back to honor his contractual obligation, because that's what you do when you sign a contract, yet he still promised that he would honor what he said. In an added step, Dan set up a fund to help all the people fired by Cumulus for refusing to get the vaccine for medical or religious reasons. One of these conservative hosts was Dale Jackson on WVNN in Alabama. Dale took to Twitter to claim Dan wasn't backing up his words but invited Dan on the show. Dan accepted the invitation and in an epic segment, told him exactly the way it was and that he meant what he said. Dan had spoken about it on our show, and as one who likes to keep thematics up with whatever the topics are on the show, I bumped into the next segment with "Sweet Home Alabama." Dan picked up on that and gave a shoutout to our Alabama "friend," Dick Johnson, as Dale Jackson came to be known. Now we play "Sweet Home Alabama" once a week in our weekly ode to Dick Johnson. (After a heartfelt shoutout to Dan wishing him the best on the second anniversary of the show, Mr. Jackson has mended fences with Dan, and Dale Jackson is our official Alabama representative as the Duke of Dothan, the Monarch of Mobile, the Baron of Birmingham, and the Aristocrat of Auburn, with other possible titles pending.)

2. THE PANTERA INCIDENT

When we first started to prepare the show to go on the air, we had to develop all the production elements from scratch. We needed a production library, I had to write liners, we needed a show intro, and so on. We also needed bumpers—that's the music we rejoin the show with from the commercial breaks. Mike and I put together over three hundred of these. We use a lot of songs that you know and others you may not know but that I think sound good rejoining a show. Early on, in the first months of the show, if Dan didn't like one of the bumpers (I didn't really know his taste in music yet), he'd call it out on the air and say he didn't like it. I'd play a record scratch sound effect and purge the bumper from the system, humanely of course, and it would never be heard from again. One of these bumpers was Pantera's "Cowboys from Hell." Pantera is a heavy metal band from Arlington, Texas, that has a large, passionate fan base. They only became more beloved when the band's icon, Dimebag Darrell, was shot and killed by a deranged fan as his other band, Damageplan, started a show in Ohio. Darrell was considered one of the great metal guitarists of all time, and his memorial service was attended by thousands of fans and many guitar legends including Eddie Van Halen. So I play the Pantera bumper coming back into one of the bottom of the hour short breaks, and Dan says on the air, "What the hell is that?" I told him it was Pantera, and he said, "I like heavy stuff, but that's even too heavy for me. Go ahead and get rid of that one."

When we got to the break, I told him down the line, "You're gonna hear it about that one."

He kind of brushed it off and went on doing what he was doing. When the show ended, Dan had a doctor's appointment. As we've mentioned, Dan reads your Facebook messages all the time. When he got to the doctor and was sitting in the waiting room, his messages were raging against him for disrespecting Pantera. The messages were in the high hundreds, maybe thousands, just raking him over the coals. The next day, one of the first things he says to me is, "Holy shit, you were right about that Pantera bumper. I got lit up on Facebook!" He went on the air and made a public apology and decided we would be playing Pantera once a week to atone for this egregious error in judgement.

3. THE FLO RIDA INCIDENT

I try to mix up the genres of music to have a nice eclectic sound to the show. Dan being from Florida, I made one from Flo Rida from a song of his I liked called, "Good Feeling." It's got a sample in it from Etta James that I just love, and it's just a great summer song in my opinion. I play the bumper, Dan looks up, eyes wide open, and says, "What are we at a rave or something? What the hell is that? We need to get rid of that one." So I hit the record scratch, expecting to send it to the well of souls where all the other deceased bumpers meet their eternal reward. During the break, Facebook messaging strikes again, and

Dan gets rolled by the listeners telling him he's made a huge mistake. He apologizes on the air and says it's okay to play it when I want. I didn't play it for several months, and someone messaged Dan, "You should play some Flo Rida since you're from Florida." So he tells me to play the Flo Rida, but he does a long segment on whatever content he's picked for that day and probably forgets all about it. I bump into the next segment with "Good Feeling," and Dan says, "What are we at a rave or something? What the hell is that?" Same exact thing as the first time. When I tell him it's Flo Rida, he remembers he said exactly the same thing. We all laughed about it, and once again he apologized. I have yet to play it again, but I think I may have to go for the trifecta.

4. THE ZZ TOP INCIDENT

Dan will be the first to tell you he's not up-to-date on pop culture references. As a matter of fact, I am amazed by his unique ability to remember very obscure references in very obscure movies or TV programs yet doesn't know the most popular pop culture references. On July 28, 2021, ZZ Top bassist and Rock & Roll Hall of Famer Dusty Hill died. When I produce a show, I like to play bumpers that fit the mood, go with the theme of the show, or honor someone who has passed. I don't ever tell Dan what I'm going to play, I just play it. Coming out of the bottom of the hour on the day Hill died, I played "Tush," a song Hill sang lead vocal on and was ZZ Top's first top twenty hit, and I just happened to have that bumper made. I play the bumper and the liner, and Dan says, "Hey Jim, we should play some ZZ Top in honor of the passing of Dusty Hill," to which I inform him I am currently playing ZZ Top at this very second. He had no idea. Dan and his battle with pop culture continues to this day.

5. THE CHUNKY PEANUT BUTTER INCIDENT

On Fridays, we do a segment called "Questions for Dan." You can go to Dan's Truth Social or Locals account and respond to Dan's post that says, "Questions for tomorrow's show." This is a chance for you to ask anything of Dan about his past, his personal life, anything. As an editorial note here, it doesn't have to be about politics, actually, it is preferred that it not be about politics because we do the whole show about politics. Also, don't argue with the other commenters and feel free to block the trolls that come into the feed. This leads us to exactly the kind of question I'm talking about. On Truth Social, @JSpiering had a simple enough question: Chunky or creamy peanut butter? I initially put this on the sheet as a throwaway question; I thought he'd give a quick answer and move on. Little did I know that Dan had a passionate stance on peanut butter. He proceeded to make a strong stand against chunky peanut butter because, in his reasoning, you made the butter out of peanuts because you didn't want the peanuts whole. As he is giving his answer, my mind is racing, and all I could think was that he was creating another Pantera incident. My instincts were correct, as his Facebook messages lit up with strong stances defending chunky peanut butter. But this blew up beyond what outrage even the Pantera incident garnered, so much so that Dan had to make an apology hostage video, and we now have it recognized as an official incident. I did this by playing the old 1950s group The Marathons and their song "Peanut Butter" as a reminder of this horrible lapse in judgement.

6. LONELY TEARDROPS

Whenever we rejoin the show from commercial breaks, we play a musical bumper back into the show, allowing ten seconds of music so stations may run a promo or liner as we rejoin. Then, I'll play one of our show liners before Dan comes back. Typically, the bumpers are all music, because if you have lyrics running under someone talking, it can be distracting, and the message would get lost. We make one exception. Growing up, Dan's mom played a lot of music in the house. One of her favorite artists was Jackie Wilson. One day Dan asked if I could play "Lonely Teardrops" for him coming out of a break. Not having time to edit, I played it clean, lyrics and everything. Dan recounted the story of his mom and those times when Jackie Wilson was playing in the house and since then, "Lonely Teardrops" gets played once a week, the only bumper we have that we let the lyrics play.

7. JOAN JETT MONDAY

We had the Joan Jett bumpers for a while, but one day I just happened to play it as the first bumper of the day. Dan got really fired up because it was just the kind of music he needed to get him going that particular day, and since then, we start Monday out with a Joan Jett song as the first bumper of the day.

CHAPTER 7

GOOFY GLUE INCIDENTS

Everyone has a different version of what I call "the DJ dream." I call it that because I work in radio, and that's the way the dream plays out in my head, but whatever business you are in, it will play out in your head as it applies to what you do. It should actually be called a nightmare. It's the nightmare you have when you're at your job, and you're under pressure to get something done, and you're running out of time, and the thing you need to help you seamlessly finish your job seems to always be out of reach with the clock running. I call it the DJ dream because generally I'm dreaming that the song currently playing is about to run out, and I can't find the next one to play, and something keeps coming up to prevent me from either finding it or playing it. I actually have the same dream for producing a talk show; it's that we're about to go on the air, but either I can't get to the board, the board is not there, the host is not there, or some other problem has come up that will keep me from starting the show. When you have these dreams, you wake up very disturbed and unsettled—not a good way to start your day. This is what a goofy glue incident feels like.

The goofy glue incident originally happened on the 1980s TV show *Growing Pains* starring Kirk Cameron. Nobody knows exactly what it is, but it was referred to several times throughout the run of the series. Basically, the joke was that whatever the incident was, it was so horrifying, it was never to be spoken of again. We have had several goofy glue incidents on the radio show, all to different varying degrees. We'll discuss them now, never to be spoken of again hereafter.

GOOFY GLUE 1

This is not officially what could be considered a goofy glue incident because Dan didn't bring up the reference for it until the next one, but in my mind, this is the first one we had. I would say this would have been during the second month of the show. We had gone a month, and everything was going along smoothly. Then, one day, in the middle of the show, Dan couldn't hear me at the studio in Dallas. The line from Dallas to Florida was fading in and out.

Backing up, whenever we prepare the show, I have all the elements to play in Dallas—all the sound, bumpers, liners, phone calls, and my interruptible foldback (IFB). The IFB is a button I can press so I can talk to Dan down the line. You probably have seen the earpiece he wears. That's what he can hear me and all the elements through. That's why whenever he references me or asks me a question on the show, I can answer him, but you can't hear me.

I remember distinctly we had gone into a break, just like normal, and then he could hear nothing. We pieced things together by using a cell phone for me to give instructions and to let him know when elements were being played. We had to figure this out after the show.

After spending much of the afternoon on the problem, it seemed we had things fixed. The next day, the same thing happened. We had engineers going through everything: internet connections, servers, phone lines…we had people in LA, Washington, DC, Denver, all trying to work this problem. When it happened for a third day, I had Dan adjust the wire for his IFB. That fixed it. A simple wire caused the most troublesome three days you could ever have in a radio studio.

GOOFY GLUE 2: SEPTEMBER 27, 2021

Dan was doing the show from the Fox studios in New York. I had been coordinating with the Fox Nation team for about a week trying to make sure we had everything set for when Dan arrived in New York so he could just go in, sit down, and do the show. Very nice setup—they put him in what was the Gutfeld studio at that time, a very big setup that looked nice for the Fox Nation audience. He was able to record his podcast fine; the communication from the DFW studio and New York was flawless. Everything was ready to go.

Before I go into how this and the subsequent goofy glue incidents played out, it's important to know a little about our show clock. Here is brief explainer on how the breaks

45

work, as this will help you understand how the show plays on our end. The show starts every day when our atomic clock hits 12:05:30 Eastern time. You won't hear it at least until six minutes after because we are running a thirty-second delay in case the occasional caller, or even Dan, goes off the rails (so far I've had to dump Dan only twice: once when he got too comfortable talking to Chip Roy and dropped an "S" bomb, the other time when he was mid-rant and forgot he was on the radio and let a "shit show" fly). Dan will come out of the gate firing away and go for about fifteen minutes. That's where the audience hears that "Bongino" five seconds, what we call a "stinger." This leads to what we call a floating break, meaning Dan has a window to get out of the segment. That window is supposed to be between seventeen minutes after the hour to nineteen minutes after the hour. Many times, Dan pushes it to the max and will get out at twenty or twenty-one. The breaks last five minutes for the first one in the first hour and four minutes for all the others.

The hard breaks are set on the clock at specific times. In our case, we have to finish by 28:15 at the bottom of the hour and 57:20 at the top of the hour. You can keep talking all you want after that, but you will be cut off by a server connected with a satellite that has our clock settings stored on it.

The omen that something bad was going to happen started right from the jump. When I turned Dan's mic on, he was hearing himself back through his earpiece. This is very distracting for any host. What they call the "mix-minus" was not set up correctly. Mix-minus means that the host can hear the entire mix being sent to him or her but without their voice. At this point, Dan has to pull his earpiece out when he is talking, and if I'm playing elements, he can put it back in then to hear the elements I'm playing. It took a little over half an hour to figure out what the problem was. But we solved that and figured we had clear sailing for the rest of the show.

The real meltdown happened in the third hour though. I play the intro to start the show at five minutes after the top of the hour, give Dan his cue, and we're off and running. Dan has a lot of energy at this point because in essence, with people around and not being in his home studio, he's got a live audience. This was right around the time of the border patrol "whipping" Haitian migrants hoax. He starts his monologue about the hapless Alejandro Mayorkas. Dan says, "What would secure the homeland mean to you? Well, you know, secure the homeland, meaning we want to know who's in the country." Then a pause. Then the pause is longer. Then I realize he's gone. Nothing. No response. I have to make a decision. Option A: I could easily just hit the stinger and go into the first floating break, then call Dan and find out what's going on. But we're only a minute and twenty seconds into the hour at this point, so taking a break right there is not really ideal. Option B: I can grab a clip of Dan from a recent show and just play that until I figure it out. That would have been the best option, but it would have taken too long to pull that up, so that was taken off the table. Option C: Let me play some bumper music, and I'll make a phone call. Meanwhile, Dan has no idea he's off the air. At this point, we were not using Skype to be able to see each other, so I had no way to signal him. I'm just imagining him doing a show that nobody is hearing but him and the people in the studio up at Fox in New York. Not being able to see him, I immediately call his cell phone. Of course, not expecting my call, he says, "What's wrong?" I told him we lost the feed from New York. Dan gets up and gets hold of Aaron Levine, who is running the Fox Nation simulcast of the radio show and who is also in panic mode, as this will affect the Fox Nation feed too. The Fox team is trying their best to figure out what the problem was. They're on the phone with me in Dallas over what they call "the bridge," an open line that we can communicate back and forth on. They're receiving no audio from me at all. They're thinking the problem must be on my end because they've gone through all their protocols and can't see anything wrong. I know my end is fine though, so I know it's there. Meanwhile, I'm still playing some of our longer bumper music to kill time until I can work through the problem.

There was an option D that should have kicked in but didn't. I need to tell you how we're able to broadcast nationally for you to understand that. Dan is in his studio in Florida, and I'm in my studio in Dallas. For our show to get to you in whatever town you're in, we have to have a central linkup. That is in Denver. So, I have to call Denver every day and check in so they can set our show up. You should know that whenever I hit that short Bongino stinger and then you hear commercials, it's because I hit a button in Dallas that fires off a tone that starts commercials all over the country. (Technology is crazy!) I tell you this because if there are ten seconds of dead air, a silence alarm will go off in Denver, and the previous day's show will begin automatically running. In this case, fourteen seconds went by; I know because I checked the audio and nothing fired. So America got to hear four minutes of great bumpers before I went to break.

While this is happening, I'm communicating with Fox on "the bridge," listening to Dan through my board, and trying to help them work the problem. As we get into the break, Dan asks if the problem is solved, and I tell him it was not yet. Dan goes over to Aaron and asks what's happening, while I am scrambling to prepare a segment of a show from earlier in the week so we can have something on the air when we come out of the bottom of the hour. Needless to say, there would have been several blood pressure cuffs that would have gone off the charts at this time. We all had enough adrenaline pumping to power a city block if you could convert that adrenaline to electricity. Dan is waiting for word from me as to what to do. This has now been a good seven minutes of many people trying to figure out what this connection problem was.

Finally, I can hear him down the line through my board, and I let everyone know I can hear him. I tell him we're good to go, which of course caught him off guard a bit, but because he's a total pro, he just rolled with it. I played the bumper and liner back into the segment, and

Dan says, "Don't even ask what just happened there, folks, I have no idea, but that was like a catastrophic technical meltdown on Dianabol with Wheaties mixed in." He then says that "we'll call it the goofy glue incident, for those of you who watched the Seavers on that show *Growing Pains.* Nobody ever tells you what the goofy glue incident was, but they constantly refer to it. That'll be forever known as the goofy glue incident."

As we get to the bottom of the hour, of course both Dan and I want to know what happened. The answer was unbelievable: a computer reset its internal world clock, by itself, and therefore reset all the current settings shutting everything down. The next time we did shows from the Fox studio in New York, Aaron assured us there would be no clocks resetting by themselves or any further goofy glue incidents, the latter being an impossible claim to guarantee because in radio, especially with all the new technology and the connections through the internet and elsewhere, there will always be goofy glue incidents. Which leads us to…

GOOFY GLUE 3: NOVEMBER 17, 2021

Dan was live in Florida for the Patriot Awards, and he was broadcasting from the Hard Rock Cafe in Hollywood. Aaron Levine was on the scene again and made sure everything was set up correctly so we didn't have another goofy glue incident. We had been testing together from on site for a few days before the actual show to work out any possible problems. We even hired a freelance engineer to be on site to make sure everything was hunky-dory.

Another aside and some more inside baseball: In trying to sync the radio show with the Fox Nation video simulcast, we have to make sure the video matches the audio, otherwise, you get the effect of watching a foreign language film with English dubbed in for the actors, and the mouth doesn't match what you're hearing. That can be seriously annoying because you find yourself watching that and thinking about it more than what is actually being said. Additionally, trying to sync audio and video becomes more difficult with the thirty-second delay we have for the radio show. So, the Fox folks have to do this thing called a "fax out" to make this happen (not the ancient method of sending documents over a phone line). That is done with a couple of different methods, one a simple clap test (yes, just hand claps) and another with a really annoying "glass" app that makes a really irritating noise but gives the engineers a perfect way to line up the audio and video correctly.

Now let's get back to Hollywood, Florida. Everything is fine. We start the show, Dan does the first hour; there's a lot of energy and excitement because there's a huge crowd watching him do the radio show. We start hour two; everything is humming along perfectly. Dan is doing a segment, ironically, on Alejandro Mayorkas testifying before congress about Biden keeping kids in cages at the border. (I think I just figured it out! DHS is behind the goofy glue incidents! It's a conspiracy!) We're about nine minutes in, and Dan says, "I thought none of this was happening"… and he disappears. Silence. About nine seconds pass, and I hear him say one word, then he's gone again. It happened again. At least this time we're far enough into the segment where I can hit the Bongino stinger and go to break. At that point, I have four minutes and fifteen seconds to figure out what's going on. I'm trying to talk to him, and he can't hear me. As we set up before the show, I could hear all the ambient crowd noise down the line, now nothing. I get a call from Theresa, who is there in Florida, and she tells me Dan can't hear me. I said, "Yeah, I can't hear him either." I'm on the phone with engineers, on the bridge again with Fox Nation, and nobody knows what's going on. On site in Florida, engineers, IT people, and security are running around like someone kicked a fire ant mound. If you've never seen that, trust me, that's a lot of chaos going on. Unlike the last goofy glue incident, I can't give Dan cues down the phone line because I have no connection to him. This time, I had to start to pull a segment from another show while the people from Fox are scrambling to find out what is going on. I can hear the chaos happening on the bridge. They know it's on their end at this point because it was more than just one show that was being affected. Thankfully, within our commercial break window, they found the problem and re-established connection. What happened? Unbelievably, a catering truck pulled up to the loading dock where all the TV production trucks were and just decided to pull a plug so they could plug something in. Didn't ask anybody, just decided, "Hey, nobody's probably using this," and unplugged us. I talk down the line to Dan, he can hear me, I give him a countdown, hit the bumper and the liner, and Dan comes back with, "The goofy glue incident is back! Goofy glue number two!" He then told a story about when he first got into radio filling in for Hannity and being so paranoid that the show was going to go down, he had the engineer constantly checking the connection. Now after doing this for a while, he says you just kind of have to roll with goofy glue incidents.

GOOFY GLUE 4: APRIL 11, 2023

This is not an officially sanctioned goofy glue incident by the international governing body that decides goofy glue incidents, but I'm making an executive decision to include this one because it involves one of the OGs of goofy glue incidents. It also changed a major staple of the show permanently.

When I first accepted the position to produce Dan's show, one thing I was told was don't worry about guests because Dan doesn't like to do interviews. He'll tell you himself he's not good at it (although I completely disagree). I was okay with that because, believe it or not, booking guests is one of the hardest things to do on a radio show until you build up a big enough contact list. This is why networks have people specifically hired just to book guests. That's their only job. At that point, I didn't have a big list because in the previous show I produced, it was really hard to get anyone to agree to come on, or the host just rejected many of the people I suggested. The other issue is that a lot of times there are several different contacts you have to go through to get to the right person, or contacts change, or they don't get back to you for a few days, or things come up, and changes have to be made. There are a lot of issues with booking guests. So that was good. Then I have my first ever call with Dan, and one of the first things he tells me is, "I want to have a lot of guests, not every day, but almost every day." Well, it turned out we were getting guests every day. Guests can be a frightening proposition for a producer because you can do everything in your power to have their contact information and make sure they have your contact information, but until you have them on the line and know that they are going to be there to actually do the interview, your heart races and blood pressure goes up. We usually do guests at the top of the hour, and as I explained earlier, we start the segment at five minutes and thirty seconds after the top of the hour. There have been times where we were still not connected with a guest until the clock hit five after, other times where we didn't connect until after I hit the show intro, and other times where they didn't show up at all. This is very nerve-racking and causes a lot of tension. Dan does a lot of preparation for these interviews, and when they don't happen, it's a waste of time, and time is one of the most expensive commodities in the Bongino world.

On April 11, 2023, we had Kirk Cameron scheduled, the star of *Growing Pains* in the '80s and part of the absolute original goofy glue incident (whatever it was). Of course, Dan had a lot of questions for him about serious issues, as Kirk is a true soldier for righteousness in the culture wars, but of course he was going to ask Kirk to settle the mystery of the original goofy glue incident. We always supply our guests with our guest line to call in, but I always ask for a number to call in case we don't hear from them by a certain time. In this case, Kirk didn't have a number we could call because he had an issue with his cell phone and didn't currently have one. We're at two minutes after and still no Kirk. I called my contact to say we haven't heard from him. He says he'll get in touch with him. He called me back and said Kirk is in a waiting room. Now think about this: I've got less than three minutes to go, my contact is communicating with Kirk by email, and I have no way to call him. Kirk was very excited to do the interview, by the way, and had prepared extensively prior to the hit time. Apparently, Kirk was using a computer to call, because he says when he dialed the number, it took him to a Bongino podcast/radio waiting room, and he was just waiting for us to join. Well, we're just a simple old fashioned phone operation, so we couldn't access or join any waiting room. The seconds are ticking away. It was like an old cartoon where you see the hands of a clock speeding around the dial—at least that's what it looked like in my head. I've got Mike standing by, as he always is, ready to take the call, Dan in my ear asking if we're connected yet, and my contact on the phone telling me if he's making any progress with Kirk. "Have him get to any phone, a hardline, someone else's phone, anything." He wasn't able to. Five minutes, thirty seconds hits, and I hit the intro. No Kirk. We go live, and Dan's giving it a few minutes to see if we can connect. This is really an awkward situation for him because he has to choose between punting with content until we connect or scrapping it and moving on with the show. He's looking at me over Skype waiting for me to tell him if it's a go or not, and I eventually make the decision to abort. Of course, Dan's not happy, because he meticulously plans the show, and when plans go awry, it's frustrating. So, at that point Dan says, "I'm gonna make an executive decision. No more guests." This wasn't rash or coming out of nowhere, because this is the second day in a row this had happened. A guest you may know was supposed to be on the day before, but we weren't able to connect with him either, and I had the number to call him! But when he told me he was at an airport, that should have been a red flag for me. So, Dan said no more guests, a major change to a staple of the show. But we've now reached a nice medium where we have people on maybe twice a week and when it's relevant to the news cycle. But because this incident involved Kirk Cameron, the OG of goofy glue incidents, this will be unofficially recognized as goofy glue number four.

(Addendum: We tried again with Kirk and made it work! Kirk came on the show June 9, 2023, and discussed the original goofy glue incident, or should I say warned us never to speak about it. When Dan asked about the original goofy glue incident, Kirk's response was, "You don't want to know. That's how bad it is. No one talks about the goofy glue incident. In fact, those three words should rarely be uttered. I've said them more in the last minute than I have in the last thirty years." We agree Kirk. Those words should rarely be uttered, and goofy glue incidents should not ever happen.)

GOOFY GLUE 5: SEPTEMBER 15, 2023

In baseball, if you fail to get a hit seven out of ten times you're up to bat, you're considered a really good hitter. If that happens with radio shows, that's a really horrible batting average. This seems to be the pattern with our remote broadcasts. Today's technology offers the ability to do a radio show from anywhere. It also offers the ability for things to go horribly wrong.

This particular day, Dan had done a book signing in Cary, North Carolina, the day before for his latest book, *The Gift of Failure*. Little did we know that would be prescient for what we were about to experience. I had talked with the program director of WFNC the week before, and we checked our connection, made sure all was set up for the broadcast, and everything worked perfectly. The day of the show, I got to the studio early and called the station, and we connected, tested, and again, everything was perfect. I had three guests lined up for an hour-and-a-half block in the middle of the show. At the top of the second hour, we talked with North Carolina lieutenant governor Mark Robinson about his race for governor and all the cultural issues plaguing the country and what could be done about them. Everything was going great. And then....

We go into the second segment of the second hour; things start out swimmingly. We're about a minute away from the hard break kicking in, and I begin to hear this sizzling sound. At first it was some simple electrical clicks and then they started to escalate until it sounded like bacon frying. I couldn't go to commercial because we were going into the hard break, so the only thing I could do was take it to break myself. I pulled Dan's mic down right away and told the audience we were having some technical difficulties, and hopefully after the break we would have everything fixed, and that we'll have Miranda Devine on to talk about the Hunter Biden indictment. As soon as we went into break, Dan calls and says the Comrex unit overheated. A Comrex or Access unit is what we use to do a lot of these remote shows. They've become very standard for radio stations and shows across the country because they are easy to use and transport, and as long as you have an internet connection, you can do a radio show. The station had another Comrex unit and was quickly trying to set that up. They had to wait for it to boot up and then we could try to connect. The connection is made through the internet, so we had to sync IP addresses then test whether I could hear Dan and they could hear me. Mind you, we had five and a half minutes to try to get all of this done. I was listening through my cue speaker to see if I could hear anyone talking through the mic in the studio, but all I was hearing was the radio broadcast on WFNC. We're a minute out, and Dan asks what we should do. "Let me have Mike call you on the guest line, and you can do it over the phone," I said.

"No, I don't want to do that. I don't think it will sound good."

I told him, "Well, we have Miranda on the phone, and we have two choices: either you interview her from your phone, or I'll have to do it. We have thirty seconds."

Dan says, "No, I'll stay on the phone with you, and we'll see if they can get this working."

So, I play the bumper, the liner, and the problem still is not fixed, so I have to go on the radio. Dan is still on the phone, and he starts talking to me as I'm talking, so I just hold the phone up to the mic. We have Miranda Devine holding, and I tell him on the air, let's just get you on the guest line, and you can talk to her that way. He agrees, and I get both of them on the air and we're off. While Dan is doing the interview, I'm on the phone with the program director trying to figure out how to get him back. At this point, I have to completely trust that Dan remembers he's not on the podcast and can't say any bad words (still a no from the FCC) that I might have to dump. They finally get it to the point where I can hear what's coming down the microphone. We're in business, but I have to wait until the commercial break before I can see if they can hear me down the line.

He finishes the interview and calls me. I told him I could hear him and hit the button to talk down the line to him, and he said all he hears is the radio station feed. So, they were able to get his mic back working, but now the station feed I was hearing was going to him. I reminded him he had a live read, so he had to do the segment on the phone again. All he had to do was talk for this short segment and get us to the top of the hour where we would have eight and half minutes to figure all of this out. We had Vivek Ramaswamy coming up after the top of the hour too, so I really wanted to get this resolved. I could hear something low in the background and thought I was hearing the studio but wasn't sure. Paula was there with Dan, and she called and said they were still working on it. Dan wasn't in the studio, so I needed her to do a mic test for me. I don't know if you're familiar with the old Cheech and Chong bit with Dave: Cheech knocks on the door and says, "Hey man, it's me, Dave. I got the stuff, let me in."

Tommy Chong: "Dave?"

Cheech: "Yeah, man, it's me, Dave, let me in."

Chong: "Dave's not here man."

Well, I'm on the phone with Paula, and I'm telling her I need a mic test. "Paula, I need you to go to the mic."

Paula: "Mike?"

Me: "Yes, I need to test the mic."

Paula: "Mike's not here."

It's always good to find humor in dark times. I did get her to test the mic, but they still couldn't get their Comrex unit to hear what we were sending from my studio. I told Dan he was going to have to do it from his cell phone again. And things go from bad to worse when 05:30 comes, and Vivek isn't there. So, we start hour three, and Dan is on the phone doing a great job explaining what was going on when we see the guest line ring and Mike answers. It's Vivek. Finally, something goes right. I get Dan on with Vivek (I can't tell him, because he can't hear me, so I have to text him on the phone he's currently broadcasting on). Then I proceed trying to work with the program director and the engineer to figure out what the heck is going on. Keep in mind, I'm trying to run a radio show and troubleshoot technical issues from fifteen hundred miles away at the same time. The interview goes well, and we go to break, and we still don't have the feed from Dallas able to reach the studio in North Carolina. We improvise. I believe it was Paula who said, just FaceTime him. Bingo. Perfect. He wouldn't be able to hear any of my cues, bumpers, liners, or clips I was playing, but I could give him visual cues as to when to start talking. Luckily, he knew all the content and was able to pull off the rest of the show just like everything was normal. We still never figured out what the issue was, but I'm sure the History Channel will do one of those shows on it, maybe *The UnXplained* with William Shatner or the show with that alien guy with the goofy hair.

GOOFY GLUE 6: OCTOBER 12, 2023

The one thing in common with all of the previous goofy glue incidents is that they had to do with remote connections. Technically and to the true letter of the word, the way we do the show is also through a remote connection, but it was set up with different equipment and tested meticulously to avoid any problems because this is what we were going to be using on a daily basis. We also have a backup unit we can immediately go to should something go wrong. Aside from the first one where there was an equipment malfunction, the setup between Dan's studio and the studio in Dallas had been solid for two and a half years. Until....

Everything was status quo; the show was progressing like normal. I was watching Dan on Skype and in the first hour, about ten minutes into the third segment, I saw a little flicker of light, heard a beep, and I heard Dan say, "Uh oh," and the Skype was gone, and so was he. I went to break and he called immediately. "We lost power, I don't know what's going on." Gui happened to still be in the studio working on clips for the clips channel on Rumble. He said the power kept flickering on and off. The way it's supposed to work if there's a power interruption goes like this: Everything in Dan's studio is powered by a UPS battery, uninterruptible power supply. If the power goes out, the battery clicks on immediately and we don't miss a beat. It should last about an hour. If power is out for more than thirty seconds, a generator kicks on and everything will stay status quo. In this case it was chaos. A good portion of the equipment and lights in the studio kept flickering on and off. The immediate thought was that it was a breaker on the switch panel. We had an issue with it before and Gui ran to go make sure the breaker hadn't tripped. As the lights continued to flicker on and off, he kept checking the breaker, only to finally figure out that wasn't the problem.

I'm at the studio and I don't know any of what's taking place there, only that Dan and Gui are at the other end of the phone trying to figure it out. I'm nearing the end of the 4:15 break and getting ready to rejoin the show, so I tell Dan to hang up and call the studio line and we'll do the show from the cell phone, like we had to do in North Carolina. He does the short segment, and as he's doing the show on the phone, I can hear him again in the studio through my cue speaker. When we go to break at the top of the hour, I tell him I've got him back. We've got eight and a half minutes to decide what we want to do—keep doing the show on the phone or trust that we're back up and running. We decide that we'll do it live. The second hour begins, I hit the intro, Dan starts to talk, and he's gone again. I come on and explain about the technical difficulties, and we get him back on the phone. He does the rest of the first long segment on the phone. As he's talking I hear him come back, but I'm not going to make the switch until the break. Gui brings the Skype back up and it looks like we're in business. Two minutes later he's gone again. Of course, nobody is hearing this because Dan is doing the show from his phone. We are able to get the feed back up a third time, and minutes later it crashes again. When we get to the break, we decide to give it one more shot. I can hear him, the Skype is up, and before I can hit the bumper I lose him again. We call him back right away and decide we're just doing the whole rest of the show on the phone. The goofiest of goofy glues.

So what happened? The power on the island where Dan lives had a massive failure. Like I explained earlier, those UPS batteries should kick right in and give you power for close to an hour. In this case, the battery powering the radio equipment and many of the lights and one of the internet feeds had failed. It didn't have enough juice to keep everything running. That would have been fine if the power was completely out because the generator would have kicked in after thirty seconds of no power. But because it was flickering on and off, we were never able to reach that thirty seconds. We finally figured out all of this in a post-mortem after the show and now have a gameplan in case something like this happens again.

CHAPTER 8

THE BONGINO GOLDEN RULES

Dan seems to come up with a new golden rule all the time. I had to keep writing them down to keep track. The following are the Bongino Golden Rules in no particular order except for the first one, which is the most important.

BONGINO GOLDEN RULE #1: DON'T GET DEAD.

This is important for obvious reasons. If you get dead, it's really going to be disappointing to your family, and you will not be able to do your part to help keep the Republic from crumbling to the ground. Getting dead does have the advantage of you reaching your eternal reward, but it's a big negative for all of us back here on Earth. Getting dead will also prevent you from being able to follow and/or live by the rest of the golden rules. All other rules are predicated on you being able to follow this first and most important rule.

BONGINO GOLDEN RULE #2: WE SEE LIBERALS AS PEOPLE WITH BAD IDEAS; LIBERALS SEE US AS BAD PEOPLE WITH IDEAS.

The one advantage conservatives have always had has been winning in the arena of ideas. We had to develop sharp arguments to support our views and policies out of necessity. There was not media or anyone in academia or in the political class we could count on to accurately portray our beliefs, because they hate us and our ideas and will do everything to discredit them. So, we spend tremendous amounts of time and intellectual capital to develop and explain these ideas. Since the Left owns the large majority of the media space, we have to do everything we can to rise above it. And what are we met with? You're a Nazi, bigot, sexist, racist, homophobe, xenophobic phobophobe. That's the retort. Because they hate us. And since they own the media industrial complex, they don't have to develop coherent arguments because they control the message. This is not new. Since WWII they painted any real conservative, like Goldwater and Reagan, as crazy despotic cowboys who were going to get us into nuclear war. Even milquetoast Republicans like both Bushes, Mitt Romney, and John McCain were Hitler, dog killers, and cheated on their wives, respectively. And each time one of them no longer was a threat to gain power, the next one up gained the title of evil, racist Nazi. But Trump, Trump broke them all. He was able to break them all because when he won the presidency, he did all the things conservatives promised to do for decades and never did. In doing so, he not only infuriated Democrats for instituting conservative policies, but he infuriated establishment Republicans for making them look like the "all talk, no action" gutless simps that they were. He also wasn't able to be manipulated by the uniparty establishment. He had no interest in making the rounds at the DC cocktail circuit, and they hated him for it. He completely broke them because if there's one thing you don't do in Washington, DC, it's mess with their way of doing things. Because of this, now you can't have rational debates with them anymore. They'll either go to the racist trope, or if you cite a manipulated or out of context statistic or fact, they'll shout "racist," then when you ask about the completely provable fact you just presented them, like "rain is wet" for example, they will wholly discount it as coming from "Faux News."

BONGINO GOLDEN RULE #3: TO AVOID DISAPPOINTMENT, NEVER PUT YOUR TRUST IN A POLITICIAN.

This seems obvious; however, you wouldn't believe the amount of people who actually are trusting of politicians. There are very few on Capitol Hill that you can really count on the fact that they will do what they say, and they're mostly on the Republican side. How many times have we seen Republicans make promises on the campaign trail to enact all kinds of conservative policies, only to get in office and do nothing but go along with the establishment? A caveat: many if not most Democrats do what they say they're going to do, but those things are actually destructive to the Republic, and if they know it's not popular or think a bill won't pass, they find a way to get around it. A perfect example: the Inflation Reduction Act. That bill does not reduce inflation; in fact, it raises it by printing and spending even more money. But it wasn't about inflation at all. It was the unpopular Green New Deal in disguise, and of course after they passed it, they admitted it. Joe Biden in a speech in August 2023 said, "I wish I hadn't called it that. It has less to do with reducing inflation than it does providing for alternatives that generate economic growth," while not explaining what those alternatives were or how they were going to generate said growth. The EPA said, "The Inflation Reduction Act incentives reduce renewable energy costs for organizations like Green Power Partners— businesses, nonprofits, educational institutions, and state, local, and tribal organizations. Taking advantage of Inflation Reduction Act incentives, such as tax credits, is key to lowering GHG emission footprints and accelerating the clean energy transition." You know how else you can tell? Outfits like Media Matters and The Nation keep claiming the Inflation Reduction Act is not the Green New Deal. That's the biggest tell. Kind of a sub rule to this rule, let's call it section (A) set your expectations to zero for Democrats, and you will never be disappointed. You know what you're going to get every time. So why waste any neurons and axons on the thought that maybe they really do love the country and will rise up above their ideology and will do the right thing for the country? That's just not going to happen. If it is a logical, common sense, reasoned argument or policy, but its conclusion is a conservative solution, not only will they reject it outright, but they will call you a racist, sexist, homophobic, misogynistic, xenophobic phobo-phobe with no pronouns. This goes exactly to one of Dan's theories that we'll get into in the next chapter. So if you have those expectations, you will never be disappointed. And this leads us to...

BONGINO GOLDEN RULE #4: THERE ARE REPUBLICANS THAT ARE REALLY DEMOCRATS, BUT THERE ARE NO DEMOCRATS THAT ARE REALLY REPUBLICANS.

You've all seen it. When the Democrats have a bill, a policy, or a cause, they are in lockstep, all of them fall into line, and you will not be able to negotiate or convince any of them to come to the other side. But Republicans? That's easy. How many times has this happened? Republicans run, for example, on protecting Second Amendment rights, and when the Left politicizes a tragic mass shooting and immediately demonizes guns, you have people like Sen. John Cornyn and other RINOs draw up a bill to restrict your gun rights. Or even more recently, the deal on the debt ceiling—the Republicans caved on that as well, now basically giving up the debt ceiling altogether. The Trump presidency was probably the most revealing of this defect with Republicans. There were so many who teamed with Democrats to stand in the way of the Trump agenda. He ran on securing the border, building a wall, energy inde-pendence, and making America's financial interests more important than spending around the world. We had the House, the Senate, and the presidency and should have been able to accomplish a massive chunk of this agenda in the first hundred days, which is the traditional benchmark. But Speaker Paul Ryan and several RINOs slow-walked many of these policy initiatives, so basically nothing got done for two years. It was like pulling teeth to get money for the wall, even though that was one of the most popular parts of Trump's agenda. It's because once many Republicans feel the love and the admiration of media when they side with Democrats, even though the policies will hurt Americans, they get addicted to the attention in the same way people addicted to social media are addicted to likes. And that leads us to...

BONGINO GOLDEN RULE #5: IF YOU DO LIBERAL STUFF, THE APOCALYPSE HAPPENS.

You don't need to do anything more than look at the current administration. Let's look back before Biden became president. Donald Trump had arguably one of the most successful presidencies we've ever seen. First, he did what he said he was going to do when he came into office. He had a serious border policy that started with constructing a wall and a remain-in-Mexico policy. He made European countries finally pay for their own defense in NATO. The Abraham Accords were historic Middle East peace deals. We had energy independence for the first time in decades. He got rid of red tape regulations to unleash the economy. There were historic lows in unemployment. A skyrocketing stock market made Americans' 401(k)s much richer. We had no wars, there were drawdowns from places we had troops, and so much more. All this while dealing with a hostile congress, corrupt media, and made-up scandals like the Russia collusion hoax. Were it not for COVID resulting in the abuse of mail-in balloting and a media covering for Joe Biden, who was campaigning from his basement and who hid the Hunter Biden laptop story, Trump wins in a landslide. The media attacked Trump over his handling of COVID when there were Democratic governors literally sending people to their deaths in nursing homes that they ignored. So, we get Joe Biden, who reversed nearly everything Trump did on day one, and what did we get? Historic highs in inflation, bare shelves because of supply chain issues, reliance on OPEC again for oil, record spending, a wide-open border, a fentanyl crisis, a war in Ukraine, an emboldened China beating war drums, turning the FBI on American citizens, an American gulag in Washington, DC, a DOJ that is unleashed on Biden's chief political rival, Donald Trump. Nothing but absolute destruction. And to make matters worse, you have a media who not only ignores it all but tells you how great things are. They actually ran stories extolling the greatness of "Bidenomics." Historically low unemployment, they tell us. Inflation has come down dramatically, they say. Wages are up, and gas prices are down, they say. That's what they say, but it really stretches the truth. Yes, unemployment is historically low, but so is the job participation rate, as many have just given up on looking for work. Yes, inflation has come down dramatically, but from where Biden's policies drove it to forty-year highs! You can't cause 9 percent inflation with reckless and unnecessary spending measures and then brag that it's come down four points when it's still double what it was when you took office. And real prices are astronomically higher than when he was installed (yes, I purposely used that word to trigger the lefties because it's fun to do that). Yes, wages have gone up, but not enough to keep up with inflation, so people are actually losing money with each paycheck. Prices on most goods are up 17 to 22 percent, at the time of this writing, since Biden took office. And yes, gas prices are down...from the highs caused by the reversal of the Trump energy policies and the lockdowns that made fuel more scarce because it wasn't being delivered.

On the world front, they call the botched Afghanistan withdrawal, which caused the deaths of hundreds of Afghans, saw people falling off airplanes, saw the death of thirteen US servicemen and women from a terror attack, left behind hundreds if not thousands of Americans and our Afghan allies, and left behind millions of dollars in military equipment for the Taliban, an unprecedented success! Then Russia invades Ukraine, and we're sending Ukraine money and equipment, essentially putting us in a proxy war with Russia. And as of this writing, China is beating the war drums and threatening to invade Taiwan. We have Chinese and Russian fighters buzzing our aircraft and navy vessels too. All of this in a possible lead-up to World War III. Complete and utter chaos, and the man in charge most likely has to be reminded what his name is in the morning, let alone that he's the president of the United States.

BONGINO GOLDEN RULE #6: UNTIL WE START IMPOSING REAL, MATERIAL LOSSES ON THE LEFT, WE WILL NEVER WIN.

Over the decades, we have ceded so much ground in the culture war to the Left. It started with allowing the leftists to take over academia, allowing them to inject the cancer of Marxism into the brains of kids. Those kids grew up to take jobs in journalism, music, and TV and movies in Hollywood. They used those media to further spread the cancer throughout society, and we're seeing it reach critical mass right now. Who would have ever thought a Supreme Court nominee would not be able to do something as simple as to define what a woman is? It looks almost impossible to retake that ground right now, but it can be done. The Bud Light fiasco is a perfect example. They decided it would be a good idea to honor a man on the one-year anniversary of him pretending to be a woman. On the surface, one could do what we would always do, shrug it off and say, "Okay, whatever." But that's what we've done for far too long. The main consumers of Bud Light were hardworking, blue-collar people who believe in God, family, and country, those who just like to have a good time on the weekends or open a cold one after work without breaking their bank account for something "hoppy, hazy, or full-bodied." These are the people who have been getting bombarded with leftist propaganda calling them racist and homophobic, and the elites running Anheuser-Busch thought it would be a good idea to shove more of this propaganda down their throats.

Because everything in their lives was being infused with all of these different agendas, this seemed to be the boiling point. People had had enough. Bud Light got immediate backlash on social media, then people stopped buying it. Bud Light sales dropped precipitously almost immediately. By July of 2023, the bleeding had not stopped. Some headlines:

Fox News: "Bud Light sales 'showing no signs of rebounding', down nearly 30% from last year: Report—The drop in sales represents Bud Light earning over $26 million less than it did a year ago."

CBS News: "Bud Light sales fall further as Dylan Mulvaney fiasco lingers."

NY Post: "Bud Light no longer among 10 most 'liked' beers in US: survey."

Even the NY Times: "Cheaper Than Water? Retailers Try to Unload Bud Light."

The marketing executive responsible for this debacle is no longer at the company despite claims to the contrary. The Bud Light Twitter account can't post anything without getting a massive ratio (for those who don't know, a Twitter ratio is when the replies are astronomically higher than the likes, usually signaling strong disagreement with the post).

Apparently, the folks at Target weren't keeping up with the news or just completely ignored what happened to Bud

Light and, pun intended, said, "Hold my beer," and decided it would be a good idea to put clothes designed for trans children front and center in their stores. You heard that right: clothes for young children whose minds are still developing and may think they are dinosaurs at some point but will one day realize they are not. What are trans clothes for kids? Clothes that are "tuck friendly" and provide "extra crotch coverage." Of course, the fact checkers went to debunk this. AP ran a fact check saying that the "tuck friendly" and "extra crotch coverage" swimsuits came only in adult sizes, although they did come in extra small and were the only clothing labeled as such. But they point out that the kids' black swimsuit, "had a tag reading: 'Thoughtfully Fit on Multiple Body Types and Gender Expressions.'" Cute how they try to get around it, but it is obvious what it is. (This is one of the most humorous things about these "fact checkers." You can usually find deep down in the story an admission that what they are telling you is false or misleading is actually true.)

So what happened to Target? Boom. Massive drop in sales. By early June, Target was feeling the pain. Some more headlines:

> *NY Post*: "Target market cap losses up to $15 billion as shares drop again amid woke backlash."

> Fox Business: "Target shares downgraded again on sales concerns."

> *Newsweek*: "Target Loses $4B in Less Than a Week as Stock Price Continues to Slide."

Of course, all the liberal mainstream media outlets like CNN, CBS, and the rest dutifully reported that this was not the result of the pride clothing controversy but rather a general trend in retail sales being down, which is funny because these are the same people telling you how great Joe Biden's economy is! They also ignore the fact that at the same time Walmart's sales rose.

Disney, a company I was once proud to work for and thank God every day that I don't anymore, is also in major trouble. When I worked for Radio Disney, we had strict standards as to what we could put on the air and in commercials, not just from a content standpoint but also to not manipulate children as far as selling products in the same way products are marketed to adults. We had a Broadcast Standards and Practices team that went through every script to make sure we were in compliance. That's all out the window now. When Ron DeSantis proposed expanding the Parental Rights in Education Act to stop gender identity and sexual orientation being taught in the classroom beyond the third grade, the folks at Disney decided they needed to have an all-hands meeting on that. Chris Rufo, a senior fellow at the Manhattan Institute, obtained that video, and in it we see Disney executive producer Latoya Raveneau saying her team has implemented a "not-at-all-secret gay agenda" and is regularly "adding queerness" to children's programming. In one Disney Channel show called *The Proud Family*, the audience of children was lectured on how the United States was founded on slavery and that slaves built this country. As of this writing, the eight Disney movie releases pre-*Indiana Jones* lost $900 million. The Disney History Institute podcast says that attendance at Disney World parks is down 20 percent from last summer. The stock price went from a high of $203 in early 2021 to a low of $80 in September of 2023. But Disney CEO Bob Iger says everything is going to be just fine—just like that famous scene in *Animal House* where Kevin Bacon is screaming in the middle of a chaotic crowd, "All is well!!!"

These are the real material losses that will help us win in these culture war battles. There is an easy blueprint for these companies to follow, and it was put together in a master class by a man named Roger Skaer. This has become a big part of the radio show as well, as we play it from time to time as a public service for these companies and for anyone in general. It's only thirty-seven seconds, but it is the most informative thirty-seven seconds you will ever see. It's a short yet simple lesson laying out in an easy-to-read graph just exactly how much you have to fuck around to find out. If you fuck around at a ten, like Bud Light and Target did, you'll find out at a ten, which Bud Light and Target are. But if you keep your fucking around at a zero, you'll never find out, which is probably good for business. Michael Jordan knew this, famously saying, when asked why he didn't wade into any political controversies, "Republicans buy sneakers too." To see this lesson for yourself, check out Roger Skaer on X or Instagram. He's on TikTok too, but we don't endorse that, as it's a Chinese Communist Party tool to collect information on Americans.

BONGINO GOLDEN RULE #7: STOP WHINING AND GO TO WORK.

This seems like simple common sense, but in today's world, it has to really be explained. It's unbelievable, but that's where we are now in the country. Dan explained this in a rant on the radio, and this is when this became a golden rule. The trigger was Kamala Harris espousing the virtues of equity. What do those on the left really mean by equity? They mean, "from each according to their ability, to each according to their means," the absolute central tenet of communism. You have to understand, those who look forward to the communist utopia believe that everyone will work towards a cause just because it benefits the community. But in reality, if we are all getting an equal outcome, you will always have those who will not pull their weight in contributing to the end cause. This is human nature. This is the problem with looking at people as a collective and not a collection of individuals with divergent thoughts, feelings, and abilities. Any time you can ask the true Marxist believers a question like, "If I don't feel like working, why do I still get to share in the end result of other people working?" they will give you a response along the lines of, "Everyone will work because it benefits all." They don't get it. (This kind of conversation got me blocked by several socialist organizations on Twitter.)

We live in an America now where previously unthinkable socialist and communist ideas are embraced by those not only in the activist left movement but by their representatives in national, state, and local congresses and communities. Bernie Sanders, who honeymooned in the Soviet Union and has publicly embraced being a socialist (although he tries to dress it up saying he's a Democratic socialist), was almost the Democrat Party nominee for president! But of course, the Soviet-like apparatchiks in the party made sure that didn't happen because they already had Hillary Clinton groomed to be their comrade in chief. (Ironic that they rejected the true believer for the one who craved power for power's sake.)

Gen Z and, to a lesser extent, millennials, have bought into the equity lie. They really think that no matter where you start from, the outcome should be the same. Equity and equality cannot coexist. Young people need to go to work. The Democrats are all excited about Gen Z being active and motivated to get involved in the electoral process, but the sad fact of the matter is, they are currently consisted of people being run through indoctrination factories from kindergarten through college and not the products of hard work, paying taxes, and trying to raise families.

Think about the big thing that the Biden administration used to try to solidify the Gen Z voter: student loan forgiveness. Besides the fact that this is illegal (the Supreme Court told him so), it robs these youth of any chance of success going forward. As Dan has said on the radio show, "You're not fixing people's problems by paying off their kid's student loans. You're not fixing them by giving them food stamps for the rest of their lives. You're not fixing them by paying them not to work. You're not fixing anything. What you're doing is you're stealing opportunity away from them. It's not just that government spending and the welfare state are not good things, it's that they're evil. They're bad things. You understand the difference. You are stealing away the opportunity for those people to overcome adversity and learn a life skill. Life skills are the hardest skills of all. Stop bitching and moaning all day and go to freaking work. That's a life skill. 'But the TikTok video selection on my homepage today was awful, what am I going to do?' You're going to get your ass up and go to freaking work. That's what you're going to do. Go. To. Work."

BONGINO GOLDEN RULE # 8: REPUBLICANS ARE NOT THE ANSWER TO YOUR PROBLEMS, BUT DEMOCRATS ARE MOST ASSUREDLY THE CAUSE OF THEM.

This piggybacks a bit off of two of the above golden rules, but it's a stand-alone in this sense: government is never the solution. Ronald Reagan famously said in his first inaugural address: "Government is not the solution to our problem; government is the problem," and in a speech in August of 1986, "The nine most terrifying words in the English language are: I'm from the government, and I'm here to help." Conservatives believe that we are all rugged individualists, fully capable of managing our own affairs. When we see a problem, the first instinct we have is to solve the problem ourselves. The modern liberal believes that not only is government required to solve your problems, but the federal government must solve them, which if you are in Wyoming, or Iowa, or Texas, or Florida, for example, it is a long way away from Washington, DC, and all have varying issues that need to be addressed. Iowa, for example, doesn't have to worry about coastal erosion the way Florida does. This is why federalism is a genius design. By design, our federal government should be the weakest of the institutions that govern us. The Constitution is not only a skeletal framework of our government but also a list of restrictions on what it can do to its citizens. The state governments, by design, should have been the most powerful, and then you had county governments, and city governments as well to address the most local of issues. We know this is no longer the case. The federal government has usurped its granted authority and now ignores the Constitution. Another example of these competing visions was in September of 2023, and the subject was the new frontier of artificial intelligence. Ted Cruz, in an interview on CNBC in September of 2023, said the one thing that could really screw up the innovation we see with AI is the federal government messing it up, pointing out that putting AI in the hands of DC politicians is absurd, using the example that one of his colleagues once referred to the internet as "a system of tubes." But Chuck Schumer, on the other hand, had a completely different idea. "The worst alternative would be to do nothing," he said. "Our resolution in a bipartisan way is to do something and we told them there's going to be some things we do they're not gonna like. But we have no choice. AI is so deep. Even deeper than tech was when it first started." In that last part right there, you could hear the seething hatred in his voice that they weren't able to get a handle on control of the internet before people enjoyed the freedom they had when they used it. They tried with "net neutrality," another government ploy to control free speech under the guise of "fairness," but that failed. Another aside: that's what they always do—name things that are the opposite of what they actually do, like the "Fairness Doctrine," which was nothing more than another ploy to shut conservatives up.

The vast majority of those elected to Congress have no skill other than being able to convince a large amount of people to vote for them. This applies on the left and the right. You have Hank Johnson of Georgia, who once suggested the island of Guam would tip over if more people and resources would go there, and you have George Santos, who completely lied about his entire life to get into Congress, and you want these people to make decisions about your health care? No thank you. This is why this golden rule is key. RINOs go along with the establishment because they want to be in the club. Democrats are all about power. They want it, they crave it, and they will do whatever they can to get it no matter what happens to you.

BONGINO GOLDEN RULE #9: NOT EVERY BAD NARRATIVE ABOUT A CANDIDATE IS DEVASTATING TO THEIR CAMPAIGN.

Dan explains that the most damaging political narratives are the ones that change your preexisting notions of that person. Why is this important? Because when you hear something bad that would seem to torpedo a candidate or someone in office, it doesn't mean that people won't vote for them or will demand their resignation. History is littered with these people. President Trump is one of them. The media went crazy after the *Access Hollywood* tape in which Trump used some locker room language about women came out, thinking this would certainly end his campaign. Nope. No one cared. There was the Stormy Daniels alleged tryst too. Crickets. Because people had a perceived notion of who Donald Trump was after decades of exposure to him. They knew who he was and what he was about. They also knew his vice president pick, Mike Pence. Everyone is clearly aware that Pence's faith is very important to him, that he won't dine with another woman unless his wife is there. If it would have been Mike Pence on the *Access Hollywood* tape, or if it were Pence who had the tryst with Stormy Daniels, his career would have been finished.

Joe Biden had a reputation too. The media ignored who he really was and created this narrative of "The Scranton Kid," "Lunch-Bucket Joe," and "Blue Collar Biden." He was a man who could relate to the common man, to "Joe Six-Pack." He was the guy who was understanding and empathetic, even though he clearly was none of those things. His lies had been documented for years. He lied about how many scholarships he had to school, about where he finished in his class, about getting arrested trying to meet Nelson Mandela, about traveling seventeen thousand miles with Xi Jinping, about driving an eighteen-wheeler, about his house burning down, about his son being killed in Iraq, about an Amtrak worker who approached him on a train while he was vice president, about growing up in the Jewish, Puerto Rican, and black communities, and the list goes on and on. Even though he's been fact checked on these claims over and over again, he continues to lie and tell these stories. That's the part that's baked in with him. His supporters know he's a liar but give him a pass. But what's really turning Democrats and Independents against him is his supposed role as empathizer in chief. Here's a man who has refused to visit the people in East Palestine, Ohio, who have suffered through an environmental disaster even though he said he would visit. This is the man who went to Maui after the historic wildfires and said he could relate because his '67 Corvette almost burned up in a house fire that wasn't a house fire. But perhaps the most egregious showing of his lack of caring or integrity was after his disastrous pullout from Afghanistan. His carelessness led to the deaths of hundreds of Afghan civilians and thirteen American service men and women. In meeting with the parents, he again made it about him as he told the story of his son dying in Iraq, when in fact they knew that Beau Biden died from cancer at home surrounded by his family. And then, as the bodies of the thirteen soldiers were being unloaded from the plane bringing them home, he checked his watch…six times. Where the hell did he have to be? These are the types of things that influence people's evaluation of those wanting to represent them.

BONGINO GOLDEN RULE #10: YOU CAN'T JUST TALK; THE DO MATTERS.

People on social media and in person ask all the time, "What can we do?" Every time we have questions for Dan for the Friday show, there are a lot of people who ask that. It's impossible for us to answer specifically, but this golden rule speaks to that question. You've heard Dan say it a lot; he's an activist first. Talking is important. It's why he does a podcast and a three-hour radio show every weekday. You have to get the message out. But you can't stop there. You have to follow it up with actions. What are those actions? That depends on you. Each of you have certain skills or abilities, specialties in certain areas, aspirations and goals that will guide you in some way to put words into action. Dan also talks all the time about his friend Ginni Thomas who always tells him, "You are the leaders you've been waiting for." For Dan, it was resigning from the Secret Service because he did not support the policies of Barack Obama and thought they were destructive to the country. Then he ran for office and lost. Then he got into content production and became a voice millions wanted to listen to. He uses his current platform to promote candidates, stand up against things like mandates, and be politically active. If there's someone you believe in, make sure you get people to vote for that person by knocking on doors, volunteering for campaigns, and helping to raise money. Or run for office yourself. You could form groups or organizations that meet and discuss plans and ideas and get those out to the general public to alert them of your concerns and what solutions you see that could be implemented. One thing not to do is to wait on a politician to do something for you. How many times have you voted for people you were convinced were the real deal and would take action and get things done, only to watch them be seduced by the establishment and fall in line with not doing what you want but doing what they are told. But you can show up at their offices and let your voice be heard, bring people with you to let them know that these concerns are not fringe but the concerns of an entire community. Scott Presler is a perfect example of this. Here's a guy who used the reelection of Barack Obama to look inside himself to see what he could have done better to keep that from happening. He has been on a mission to register as many Republicans as he can before the next election. He goes from state to state, town to town, registering people. He started an organization called Early Vote Action that you can go to and sign up to help. There's not a single "one-size-fits-all" answer to the question of what can you do. But you just have to do.

BONGINO GOLDEN RULE #11: TREAT PEOPLE LIKE HUMAN BEINGS AND DISREGARD THEIR SKIN COLOR.

This is one of the newest Bongino Golden Rules, but it seems necessary at this point to make it an official rule, because Democrats are obsessed with skin color. The Left will look at the following paragraphs as a white man talking about black and brown issues, which actually proves everything I'm about to write correct. We are all aware of the problem with race in the country. Slavery was our original sin, but unlike the original sin we are born with (according to Christian theology), we are not allowed to forgive this, even though an estimated 640,000 to 700,000 men were killed, with many more maimed with limbs amputated and other deformities suffered. The assassination of Abraham Lincoln arguably is the worst thing that could have happened to African Americans, because he most assuredly would have handled reconstruction better than Democrat Andrew Johnson. Southern Democrats made life as hard as possible for freed slaves to integrate into society and into the political system with things like poll taxes. The KKK was founded by former Confederate general Nathan Bedford Forrest, a Democrat. Sharecropping became its own form of slavery. Jim Crow laws were put into effect by Democrat mayors, police chiefs like Bull Connor, and governors like George Wallace, and finally just about one hundred years after the Civil War, the Civil Rights Act of 1964 passed ending Democrat-imposed segregation in the South. You might notice a pattern there.

But today's Democrats practice a new kind of racism. In today's woke society, what are Democrats and African Americans doing? Reimposing segregation! But this time it's great, according to them. Here's a *New York Times* headline from June 2, 2017, in an article by Anemona Hartocollis: "Colleges Celebrate Diversity With Separate Commencements." First of all, that headline makes no logical sense. We're celebrating diversity by dividing people? Do they even think about these things before they write them down? Hartocollis writes, "From events once cobbled together on shoestring budgets and hidden in back rooms, alternative commencements like the one held at Harvard have become more mainstream, more openly embraced by universities and more common than ever before." Attitudes like this go hand in hand with the new racism leftists use in what George W. Bush called "the soft bigotry of low expectations." According to the Left, minorities cannot get ID to vote, cannot succeed at taking tests in school unless they are dumbed down, cannot get certain jobs unless the standards and qualifications are lowered, and the list goes on. Joe Biden even said black entrepreneurs can't get lawyers and accountants. And they don't see this as racist.

The great Thomas Sowell has written extensively on this. In one column from November of 2014 titled "A Legacy of Liberalism," he laid out the effects on the black family from post-slavery to after the Civil Rights Act and the "war on poverty." Sowell writes:

> "If we wanted to be serious about evidence, we might compare where blacks stood a hundred years after the end of slavery with where they stood after 30 years of the liberal welfare state. In other words, we could compare hard evidence on 'the legacy of slavery' with hard evidence on the legacy of liberals.
>
> "Despite the grand myth that black economic progress began or accelerated

with the passage of the civil rights laws and 'war on poverty' programs of the 1960s, the cold fact is that the poverty rate among blacks fell from 87 percent in 1940 to 47 percent by 1960. This was before any of those programs began.

"Over the next 20 years, the poverty rate among blacks fell another 18 percentage points, compared to the 40-point drop in the previous 20 years. This was the continuation of a previous economic trend, at a slower rate of progress, not the economic grand deliverance proclaimed by liberals and self-serving black 'leaders.'"

Black "leaders" and academics of today don't want to look into any of these statistics and solve the problem. In fact, it's very profitable for some to continue this division, no matter how harmful it is to the society as a whole. Robin DiAngelo, Ibram X. Kendi, and Nikole Hannah-Jones are all successful liberal writers, fawned over by media and academia for their terribly flawed works, *White Fragility*, *How to Be an Antiracist*, and *The 1619 Project*, respectively. All of those works start with the premise that all white people are racist, that it is in their nature, and they will help you overcome this if you just listen to them. And why do they come to that conclusion? Because they are obsessed with the color of a person's skin. They do not see a free thinking individual but have to insultingly judge each individual by skin color. That is not what we as conservatives do. We actually believe that given the same opportunities, they can become great successes as many have and continue to do.

Meanwhile, those on the left can say racist things and no one bats an eye. These are actual quotes from our current president, Joe Biden:

> "Poor kids are just as bright and just as talented as white kids."

> "Unlike the African American Community, with notable exceptions, the Latino Community is an incredibly diverse community with incredibly diverse attitudes about different things."

> About Barack Obama: "You got the first mainstream, African American who is articulate, bright and clean, a nice-looking guy. That's a storybook man."

> "If you have a problem figuring out if you're for me or Trump, then you ain't black."

> "You can't go into a 7-Eleven or a Dunkin' Donuts unless you have a slight Indian accent."

That's some pretty racist stuff right there. Here's another example of how the Left must push the race narrative despite proven success that has moved past it from today's headlines. An NBC News Tweet on Sept. 9, 2023: "If Coco Gauff pulls the upset win at the U.S. Open, she'll be the latest Black American woman to leave a history-making mark on the most sacred grounds of U.S. tennis." It's not history-making at all. As Kevin – Classical Liberal in the replies pointed out, "Since 1999, 11 of the Women's US Open championships have been won by black women (Serena & Venus Williams, Sloane Stephens, and Naomi Osaka)." That's eleven champions in twenty-four years. It's not history-making. It's just normal. And here's the thing, their skin color had nothing to do with their performance.

Conservatives do not think like this. We believe in the what the founders wrote in the Declaration of Independence, that "all men are created equal." I think I recognized above that it took a long time to live up to those words, but we are at a place today where they are more achievable than ever. It is insulting and racist to reduce a person to the color of their skin. They supposedly honor Martin Luther King Jr. but spit on his dreams, those being "that one day on the red hills of Georgia, the sons of former slaves and the sons of former slave owners will be able to sit down together at the table of brotherhood...that my four little children will one day live in a nation where they will not be judged by the color of their skin but by the content of their character."

BONGINO GOLDEN RULE #12: EVERYONE YOU ELECTED TO CONGRESS HATES YOU.

This is some tough medicine to take, but you have to learn this and commit this to your brain. The people you elect are not there for you. Sorry to tell you, but they are not. Don't get infatuated with one of these members because you saw them give a barn burner speech at CPAC. You have to look at them as tools—not tools in the Jim Acosta or Keith Olbermann sense, but tools as in useful items to get something done, and in this case, they are the tools we have to drive a conservative agenda forward because that is the way you make life better for everyone. One of the big problems we have is that we look at our guy or gal in our district and say, "Yeah, they're good; it's everyone else that's screwing it up for us." No, you're invested in the personality at that point. Look at what they do. Is the tool useful in pushing conservatism? Then keep it. If it's not, then it's broken, and you have to get a new one. If there is a person running in your district that you really can't stand, has no personality, is a jerk to people but is doing conservative things, that's the tool you want to use. You must realize that if you put your faith in politicians on Capitol Hill, you're getting the double-barrel middle finger. You're going to get screwed. It's that simple. You've seen it happen election after election. You put them in office expecting conservative things, and they don't deliver. They're not there for you. But you can make sure that you have the right tools in place to make sure what you want gets done.

CHAPTER 9

DAN'S THEORIES

Besides the golden rules, there are theories that Dan has developed over the years. Though he's not a trained scientist in the academic sense, he has had enough education to observe what is going on around him and formulate reasons for why certain things happen the way they do. The Museum of Natural History in New York (my favorite place to go in the city) defines a theory as "a well-substantiated explanation of an aspect of the natural world that can incorporate laws, hypotheses, and facts. A theory not only explains known facts; it also allows scientists to make predictions of what they should observe if a theory is true…. The longer the central elements of a theory hold—the more observations it predicts, the more tests it passes, the more facts it explains—the stronger the theory." I think you'll find that these theories continually pass muster and hold up over time.

1. THE DIPSY DO FLIPEROO THEORY.

As you can already surmise, Dan put a lot of work into coming up with the proper verbiage that cuts right to the core of the theory and describes it perfectly and succinctly. The Dipsy Do Fliperoo Theory is simply this: when liberals accuse conservatives of doing a thing, the thing they are accusing them of is what they themselves are actually doing. They do this all the time. I asked Dan once what was the perfect example of this theory. He didn't even have to think about it. Russiagate. For years we had to suffer through the Russia collusion hoax. Without relitigating it, it started in 2016 when the *New York Times* started coming out with stories about the Steele Dossier, hookers in a hotel peeing on Donald Trump, secret meetings between Mike Flynn and the Russians, and so on. And it's funny; I distinctly remember these stories seemed to come out in the *New York Times* and the *Washington Post* at 6 p.m. EST every Friday for a while, like clockwork. The things they had in common were they all relied on anonymous sources, and they were all written by the same people: Maggie Haberman, Jo Becker, Matt Apuzzo, Rosalind Helderman, Tom Hamburger, Ellen Nakashima, Adam Entous, Greg Miller, and Mark Mazzetti. Why would I name those people? Because in 2018, they all won the Pulitzer Prize for National Reporting! Amazingly, still at the Pulitzer website they have the award posted rewarding the "Staffs of The New York Times and The Washington Post For deeply sourced, relentlessly reported coverage in the public interest that dramatically furthered the nation's understanding of Russian interference in the 2016 presidential election and its connections to the Trump campaign, the President-elect's transition team and his eventual administration." Wow! That seems like a big deal! Except none of it was true. They won a Pulitzer for lying. Hilariously, a March 2019 article in the very same *New York Times* written after the Mueller Report came out titled, "Mueller Finds No Trump-Russia Conspiracy, but Stops Short of Exonerating President on Obstruction." We learn that, "The investigation led by Robert S. Mueller III found no evidence that President Trump or any of his aides coordinated with the Russian government's 2016 election interference, according to a summary of the special counsel's key findings made public on Sunday by Attorney General William P. Barr." That article was written by Mark Mazzetti, one of the people awarded the Pulitzer. Amazing.

So, what was actually true? The Durham Report that came out in May of 2023 was devastating to the lies that those two supermarket tabloids told. It was Hillary Clinton all along colluding with the Russians to dig up dirt on Donald Trump! The dipsy do fliperoo! According to the *Wall Street Journal* Editorial Board on May 16th of 2023, "The report lays out numerous examples of the FBI ignoring evidence that it was being used by the Clinton campaign to execute a political dirty trick. This included intelligence the government received in July 2016 alleging that Mrs. Clinton had approved 'a proposal from one of her foreign policy advisors to vilify Donald Trump by stirring up a scandal claiming interference by the Russian security services.' Former CIA director John Brennan briefed this material to President Barack Obama, Vice President Joe Biden, Attorney General Loretta Lynch and Mr. Comey, yet the FBI ignored it. It did the same when it learned that collusion dossier author Christopher Steele was working for the Clinton campaign and that Mr. Steele and oppo-research team Fusion GPS were spreading disinformation to the press. And it ignored exculpatory statements made by Messrs. Page and Papadopoulos in secret FBI recordings." Durham's conclusion in the report itself said the investigation into Trump never should have been taken up. According to the report, "Indeed, based on the evidence gathered in the multiple exhaustive and costly federal investigations of these matters, including the instant investigation, neither U.S. law enforcement nor the Intelligence Community appears to have possessed any actual evidence of collusion in their holdings at the commencement of the Crossfire Hurricane investigation."

Another prime example is the first Trump sham impeachment. Sham? Oh, yes! Many seem to forget that the whole process was started by a "whistleblower" who claimed that Trump demanded a quid pro quo from the new Ukrainian president Volodymyr Zelenskyy, that he "withheld military aid" from Ukraine unless they dug up dirt on Joe Biden on the first phone call President Trump had with him. Adam Schiff famously lied in his statement during an intelligence committee hearing and completely made up a false story about how the phone call went. He alleged that Trump wanted Zelenskyy to make up information about Joe Biden. There are a few things wrong with this whole story, and this is how we get to the dipsy do fliperoo. The military aid was given to Ukraine on time and when promised. A *USA Today* fact check on Nov. 13th of 2019 looking into whether Schiff lied from his position as chairman of the committee goes exactly the way fact checks nearly always do; they try to run cover for Schiff, but in the article, they actually tell the truth. In this case, Lori Robertson says, "Schiff said in his opening statement, and in TV interviews, that Trump had asked Zelensky to 'make up' or 'manufacture' dirt on Trump's potential 2020 opponent, former Vice President Joe Biden. That's not accurate. Trump asked Zelensky to investigate, not provide false information." Why did Trump want Zelenskyy to investigate? Probably because he knew about Joe's quid pro quo with Ukraine. Whoa! Wait, what?? In the immortal words of Warner Wolf, let's go to the videotape! There we see Joe Biden on stage at the Council on Foreign Relations saying, "And I was supposed to announce that there was another billion-dollar loan guarantee. And I had gotten a commitment from Poroshenko and from Yatsenyuk that they would take action against the state prosecutor [Viktor Shokin, the one investigating the company Hunter Biden was working with]. And they didn't.

So they said they had—they were walking out to a press conference. I said, nah, I'm not going to—or, we're not going to give you the billion dollars. They said, you have no authority. You're not the president. The president said—I said, call him. (Laughter.) I said, I'm telling you, you're not getting the billion dollars. I said, you're not getting the billion. I'm going to be leaving here in, I think it was about six hours. I looked at them and said: I'm leaving in six hours. If the prosecutor is not fired, you're not getting the money. Well, son of a bitch. (Laughter.) He got fired."

Well, son of a bitch. Dipsy do fliperoo.

2. THE WALKING DEAD THEORY.

For those who are fans of *The Walking Dead*, you can skip the next few sentences, as I need to explain it for those who have never seen it. *The Walking Dead* is a comic book developed by Robert Kirkman and was made into a wildly successful TV show on the AMC network. It's about a virus that infects the brain, and when you die, you become a zombie that craves nothing but food constantly, and that food is people, or any living organism, except plants of course. There are no vegan zombies. The brain continues to work as the body rots away, and the only way they are stopped is by something sharp going into the brain. The story is more about the people who survive the zombie apocalypse and how they interact.

Another aside: *The Walking Dead* is one of the best shows that confirms conservative ideals that has ever been put on television (and this will really piss them off), specifically the Trump agenda: walls work; being armed is crucial for survival and defense; things that want to harm you don't care if you're trans or gay, you're just food; there are always outside threats that want to do harm to you and don't care about what you think about pronouns; having children instead of aborting them is the key to survival of humanity; law and order are crucial to a functioning society against outside threats; health care is not a fundamental right; skilled jobs like farmers, plumbers, electricians, and so forth are way more important than gender studies; it's important to know who you're letting into your community, so you create borders that you defend relentlessly.

In season three, the featured group in the story led by Sheriff Rick Grimes stumbles upon a prison. They actually go inside and clear it out to make a home for themselves. Yes, they go inside a prison to live to keep them safe from what's outside. Who would willingly put themselves in a prison? People who are afraid of what's outside. This is what we experienced during COVID. I can distinctly remember when Trump declared, "Fifteen days to slow the spread," that this was a dangerous step to take, because I knew from experience that when you give the government power, it's really hard to get it back from them. In fact, it almost never happens. This was a fatal mistake but at the same time shined a spotlight on the Left's totalitarian plan. These leftist world leaders and unelected bureaucrats at organizations like the CDC, NIH, and WHO saw their opportunity and they took it. Then they kept pushing to see how far they could go. So, in March of 2020, they told us to walk into the prison.

We all bought into it because we didn't know how bad this virus was. We were told it came from nature, jumping from a bat to a pangolin to a human, or something ridiculous like that. We were told it could kill millions in this country alone. Our elected officials were no longer running the country. Anthony Fauci, Deborah Birx, Robert Redfield, and Tedros Adhanom Ghebreyesus at the WHO were running the country and the world. Stay home; don't have friends or family over; don't go to work; if you have to go to the grocery store, stand six feet away from any other person. First it was don't wear a mask, then it turned to wear not only one mask but two. Offices shut down, schools shut down, restaurants shut down, retail stores, anything that wasn't deemed "essential." Their terror campaign was working better than they ever could have dreamed! They told us to go into the prison, and we went willingly and enthusiastically...at first. March 16, 2020, marked the start of the fifteen days.

It didn't take long for the doubts to start. The fifteen days came and went, and the lockdowns didn't end. In fact, Dr. Fauci said we needed another thirty days, and the administration went along. After the "forty-five days to slow the spread" showed it was not working, some states had had enough and opened back up. Others, mostly the ones controlled by leftists, kept the lockdowns in place. Not only that, they mandated masks be worn wherever you went outside. They even recommended that you wear them inside your home. Parks were closed, beaches were closed. The police state went into full effect. People were arrested for not wearing masks; one man was famously arrested for paddleboarding by himself, surrounded by no one in the ocean. We had willingly walked into the prison, and now they were going to make sure we stayed there whether the science supported these actions or not.

The evidence that these steps were unnecessary started to show itself. The high death rates were shown to be mostly in the elderly over seventy-five years old or in people with four or more comorbidities. Then we found out many of the treatments they were giving were not only not helpful but in many ways harmful. If you were watching, you could see the madness unfolding before your eyes. They would put people in hospitals on respirators, but nearly all of those people died. But the auto companies were recruited to turn their operations into respirator makers. We began to see that the states that went back to normal saw a statistically insignificant increase in cases compared to the states that stayed locked down. Sweden, which was completely ignored because they didn't do any lockdowns or obey any suggested COVID protocols, saw no greater increases in cases or deaths than anywhere else. And our leaders had no idea what they were doing. Governors like Andrew Cuomo and Phil Murphy were sending infected elderly into nursing homes and locking them down causing COVID to spread and kill many of these elderly people.

The fear campaign had terrible results. Many businesses that closed for the "fifteen days" never reopened. The ones that were struggling were bailed out by the government through the Paycheck Protection Program, which amounted to printing trillions more dollars for "loans" that didn't have to be paid back. We were further divided into factions. There were those who wore the mask and those who figured out they didn't work. "Mask Nazis" would publicly shame you if you were in a store not wearing a mask. I remember a personal experience of being chastised for being in the grocery store not wearing a mask. I got within six feet of a guy wearing one in the meat section, and he actually got mad at me because I was close to him.

Time went on, and fewer people bought into the danger, because it was clear things were not as bad as we were told. We were making our way out of the prison. So, then we had the Delta variant that pushed us back in. "It's even more deadly than the original COVID," they said. I'm not trying to downplay that either. There's a good chance the first time Dan got COVID, it was Delta, and it was really bad. But he didn't miss a day of work. My wife got it and was in the hospital for eight days! But I think it was the treatments that prolonged it. Those of us who resisted were pilloried even more. When many of us wouldn't comply, they brought out the Omicron scare. "It's not as deadly, but you're definitely going to get it because it's so contagious," they said. When respected doctors like Scott Atlas publicly said that, according to the *New York Times*, "The virus is overblown, the number of deaths is exaggerated, testing is overrated, lockdowns do more harm than good," he became a pariah. Others, like the most published and peer-reviewed cardiologist in world history, Dr. Peter Mc-Cullough, touted alternative and affordable treatments like hydroxychloroquine and ivermectin, which seemed to ease the COVID symptoms, and were marginalized and suddenly considered quacks. You see, the Faucis and the Birxes weren't interested in helping people get better, they loved the power. They loved keeping you in the prison. They were going to push lockdowns, masks, and social distancing because it was a way to control you, and you using alternative, widely available treatments was unacceptable. And natural immunity? Fuhgedaboutit! You're crazy. They collectively sounded like Tiffany Gomas: "That motherf***er back there is not real!"

But we eventually started coming out of the prison. We could see the light, and we were no longer afraid. Do you think they were going to give up the control they had just abused you with? Hell no! Here's another big clue that it wasn't about controlling the virus, it was about controlling you: President Trump had green-lighted Operation Warp Speed to speed the development, manufacturing, and distribution of a COVID vaccine, bypassing much of the trials and red tape usually associated with the development of new treatments. But he was also running for reelection, and those who loved the lockdowns and mandates hated him and were doing everything they could to make sure he didn't win. So, conveniently, the news that a vaccine was ready to go was released after Trump lost the election, because had those trials been completed before the election, he might have won. They used Warp Speed just fast enough to not have results before the election, because defeating Donald Trump was more important than your life.

And speaking of that election, they used the COVID fear to push mail-in balloting everywhere. Some states, like Pennsylvania, violated their own constitution to push this scheme. The whole scheme was exposed in Dinesh D'Souza's *2000 Mules* showing how using geotracking exposed ballot mules stuffing ballot boxes. Of course, the critics said the movie is not accurate because geotracking is unreliable, unless of course you're using it to find out where January 6th protesters were, then it's totally reliable.

So they had this vaccine now, so you would be left alone and be able to make your own decisions on your safety again, because something was now available to be able to stop the spread of this virus, right? Are you kidding? Do you think you're getting out of the prison that easy? No. We're going to have your employer mandate that you get the shot, or you don't have a job anymore. But what if you want to see the results of people taking it before you make the decision to? No, roll up your sleeve. But there are therapeuticals I can take that will help me get over it much more quickly; can I just use those? No, take the jab.

But what if it has some really bad side effects? It doesn't. It's perfect. Roll that sleeve up.

But what if my doctor doesn't think I should take it? He's a quack. Let's find a good vein. But what if I have natural immunity? Are you some kind of nut? Take the shot.

But does it work?

We don't care. Take. The. Shot.

Or you don't get to work. Or you can't eat here. Or you can't shop here. Be afraid. Get back in the prison.

And here's the really evil part. The NIH now lists ivermectin on its page for COVID-19 treatment guidelines. It says, "Ivermectin is an anti-parasitic drug that is being evaluated to treat COVID-19." And now the Mayo Clinic has approved hydroxychloroquine for use in COVID treatment. On its page, it says, "Hydroxychloroquine may also be used to treat coronavirus (COVID-19) in certain hospitalized patients." They go on to say that if used alone or with certain other medicines, it may increase your risk of heart rhythm problems. Fair enough, but these are the same people who pretend there has been no data showing that there are serious side effects from the mRNA vaccines.

These leftist leaders really think they're going to push it on us again! Mid-2023 they started with "a new variant is coming," talking about bringing masks back even though it's been scientifically proven they have little to no effect in preventing transmission of this virus. But they're running into a stronger wave of opposition. So that means they'll just stop and say, "Hey, our bad. Just go on about your lives." Of course not! Now they're going to spring the "climate crisis" on you.

If you were living where you are now around twenty thousand years ago, you'd be doing a hell of a job being alive, because there's a good chance where you live now was buried under ice, in some places a mile thick. Then, things got warmer, and the ice began to recede. And you know what? Things got better. Plants grew, animal life became more abundant, and early man was able to thrive because there were more food sources. Then they were able to migrate all over the planet. If you go to the Southwest, you will see the beautiful natural monuments the receding ice left us. But we're supposed to worry about rising sea levels and more severe hurricanes. Let's keep it real: Because of the shifting of tectonic plates and the ever-changing nature of the Earth to its core, a land mass we now call Pangea has broken apart into the continents we currently have. Sea levels may rise but then we migrate to where it is dry. The current coasts we have weren't always where they are. There are seashell fossils in the Rocky Mountains and in rivers in Texas, because they were once coastline! The Sahara Desert was once a tree-filled forest; Greenland was once ice-free enough for farming. There is no evidence that hurricanes are getting stronger or that these are "the hottest summers on record." The 1930s and 1950s paralleled what is going on now. Hurricanes are not getting stronger; in fact, on the list of the strongest hurricanes to hit the US, only two of the top twenty have come after 1992: Andrew in 1992 and Charley in 2004. I bet you think Katrina was a Category 5 monster. No, it was Category 3 when it hit land. The damage done to New Orleans was because the neglected levee system failed. The point is, these events have happened for millennia, and we will adjust and adapt as necessary.

All that being said, you need to look for the signs and prepare for what they will hit you with. They are trying to control every aspect of your life: no more oil, no more gas, no more gas stoves, no more plastic straws, no more plastic bags, no more incandescent light bulbs…that's all happening now. But they saw they could control you during COVID, and they're going to go for more. They will try to control how much you can drive, where you can go, how much food you can buy, what kind of food you can buy, how much power you use in your home; if they think you shouldn't have firearms or decide you have too much ammo, they'll put a stop to that, and so on. How will they do it? They will totally try to implement digital currency. When you don't have cash to pay for things, the entity that controls your bank account will have all the power. They will decide if you are spending too much on certain items or if you can even buy that item at all. They'll start with gun and ammo purchases, and it will progress from there—all in the name of "saving the planet," which is not in any danger at all. It's survived way bigger calamities in its history. But you need to get back in the prison.

But why would they want to do that? Don't they know that we have God-given rights to life, liberty, and the pursuit of happiness? Those on the left do not believe that. To them you are not a free-thinking individual of the human race; you are chattel. They hate people. That's it, plain and simple. To them, people are the problem. And not just any people. If you are not in that high elite world that went to Harvard or Oxford or has joined any of these dubious world bodies like the World Economic Forum (WEF) or the Aspen Institute or the other major organizations or are a member of the political class that runs the governments that are designed to organize your life, you're not a person; you're a thing to be controlled. Why do you think they are going after carbon dioxide as a pollutant? Because it's what we breathe out of our mouths! Think about that: they're trying to convince you that the very act of you breathing is polluting the planet. Why do you think they're so radical about wanting to abort babies? Because it is the prime sacrament in their religion. And if you make the mistake of having the child, they will do everything they can to convince that child they are not the gender they were born. Do you remember the 1968 book *The Population Bomb* by Paul Ehrlich? The whole premise was that the planet was becoming too crowded, and we were depleting all our resources, which will lead to mass starvation all over the planet. How did those predictions come out? This is not to say that we shouldn't be good stewards of the resources we have, and the water we drink, and the air that we breathe, but we still should be able to live our lives as free, rugged individuals. That's not the mindset of the Left. Remember, you're deplorable, clinging to your God and your guns. You must be kept under their control, because you're too stupid to figure things out on your own. So, they will make sure you stay in that prison.

3. THE CANNIBALISM THEORY. EVENTUALLY, WHATEVER THE LEFT IMPLEMENTS WILL CAUSE IT TO EAT ITSELF.

Dan often echoes the great Herb Stein, saying, "Whatever can't continue, won't." He uses that quote in a lot of different contexts, but it also applies itself to this theory. The Left sets up so many bars and moves so many goalposts and creates so many rules, it's hard to keep up. And eventually those bars, goalposts, and rules will overlap so that even though the lefties are trying so hard, going out of their way to comply with all these new norms, they're going to violate one of them. That's when they begin to eat themselves. Because you must comply with all of them.

Remember during COVID seeing all the "stop Asian hate" signs and news stories on attacks against Asians? This was supposed to be the virtue signaling against "white supremacists." You see, the white supremacists were on the march for any person of Asian descent because Donald Trump kept calling COVID, "the China virus," and that was a dog whistle to the Proud Boys and the Oath Keepers to hunt Asians wherever they could find them. Of course, that wasn't true, and when Asians were attacked, the attackers were ignored, because it turned out white supremacists weren't attacking them. But those on the left were so concerned about what was happening to Asians in the country, except when it came to opportunities in higher education. It seems the food pyramid of leftist hierarchy has Asians at the bottom. Because their culture requires work ethic and laser focus when it comes to education, they got very high grades and finished at the top of their class, and that put them in line for admission to some of our most prestigious institutions. And did all that hard work pay off? Of course not. Places like Harvard had to meet certain racial quotas, regardless of grades or academic achievement. This wasn't classified as Asian hate—it wasn't discrimination; this was just fair. So, of course, some of these Asian families were quite upset when, after the years of hard work and dedication they put in to be at the top of their class in high school, they were passed over for admission consideration by Harvard for someone who had lesser academic achievements;

but what they did have was the correct skin color. That was the case brought by Students for Fair Admissions, an organization founded by legal activist Edward Blum, who said, "What is happening on college campuses today is that applicants are treated differently because of their race and ethnicity. Some are given a thumbs up. Some are given a thumbs down," according to an article in October of 2022 by NPR. The case also considered the admission policies of the University of North Carolina, because it was a state school, and Harvard was a private school. The Supreme Court ruling came out in June of 2023 and overturned "affirmative action," with Chief Justice John Roberts writing in the majority opinion, "Eliminating racial discrimination means eliminating all of it," and in a concurring opinion, the Left's most hated Supreme Court justice, Clarence Thomas, wrote, "The Constitution continues to embody a simple truth: Two discriminatory wrongs cannot make a right." Thomas is hated because he is a black man who actually thinks for himself and refuses to bow down to liberal orthodoxy.

So, the Left lost their collective minds. In the *New York Times*, Adam Liptak lamented, "The decision all but ensured that the student population at the campuses of elite institutions would become whiter and more Asian and less Black and Latino." Joe Biden made a speech on the ruling saying, "Discrimination still exists in America. Today's decision does not change that." Actually, it did, Joe. It literally stopped discrimination. The next day on *CBS Mornings*, they brought on former president of Brown

University Ruth Simmons, who compared the ruling to *Plessy v. Ferguson*, the famous "separate but equal" ruling in 1896 that codified segregation. Two days after the ruling, protests started at Harvard. *Harvard Magazine* described it like this: "Led by the Coalition for a Diverse Harvard, more than 100 students, alumni, and members of the public united in opposition to the decision, gathered at the John Harvard statue and marched to the Science Center Plaza, to the Smith Campus Center, and back. As some organizers distributed pins and purple t-shirts reading 'Our Unity is Our Strength, Our Diversity is Our Power,'" not having it dawn on them they were protesting in favor of discrimination. And in a moment that showed a total lack of self-awareness, Joy Reid went on MSNBC and said, "Let me just be clear. I got into Harvard only because of affirmative action." Case closed.

Then there is the recent story of Ibram X. Kendi, the author of *How to Be an Antiracist*, in which his answer to that is to be racist. Kendi had an antiracist research center at American University, and shortly after the George Floyd riots, he was hired by Boston University and moved the center there. In his founder's statement, he said, "It is being built as the fight against racism takes center stage in American life…. We must be willing to do the hard research and policy and narrative and advocacy work to bring about change. We are willing. Let's build the BU Center for Antiracist Research. Encourage us, support us—help us build the world anew." Twitter's Jack Dorsey was so moved that he gifted the center $10 million with no strings attached. That's virtue signaling with a lot of zeroes in it. Kendi thanked him for his generosity on Twitter saying, "Your $10M donation, with no strings attached, gives us the resources and flexibility to greatly expand our antiracist work. The endowment is vital, as we build our new Center." That was back in 2020. Fast forward to September of 2023, and it seems Mr. Kendi may have lost his way. After $43 million in grants and gifts, which produced very little research, around 40 percent of the staff was laid off, and of those disgruntled employees, they accused Kendi of mismanagement of funds and creating a toxic culture in the center. One BU professor called the layoffs an "act of employment violence and trauma [that] is not just about individual leaders. It's about the cultures and systems that allow it to occur." It was a shock for Kendi to find out his center of antiracism was infiltrated from outside! You see, Kendi's statement about the layoffs included the following: "Leaders of color and women leaders are often held to different standards and routinely have their authority undermined and questioned." Basically, his conclusion was that you can't question the lack of research or where all that money went. If you do that, you're racist and sexist. The Center for Antiracism was apparently full of racists, I guess.

But I think my favorite and the most illustrative is the story about the Grace Hopper Celebration held annually in Orlando. It's basically a job fair for women to get into the STEM arena, but 2023 made it a priority to make sure non-binary people were added into the mix as well. If you're still trying to figure out what non-binary is, *Webster* defines it as "relating to or being a person who identifies with or expresses a gender identity that is neither entirely male nor entirely female." Let's put to the side for a second that particular definition has no basis in reality or biology, but one of my favorite things to point out is that by claiming you are non-binary, you have now created a choice between binary and non-binary, therefore creating a binary situation, but never mind that; once you go down this path, you cannot deviate from it. These are the people who will defend a man's right to compete in a competition that is exclusively for women, a word they can't—or refuse to—define by the way. They will tell you that you cannot keep these men claiming to be women, whatever that is, from undressing in the women's locker room, showing their junk. These young women, who have been practicing at their particular sport since they were young, with dreams of doing great things, were now losing to men pretending to be women, and you better accept it dammit.

So, when in 2023 a whole lot of straight men decided they wanted access to these companies as well declared themselves to be non-binary, well, the lefties who organized this collectively lost their minds. AnitaB is the organization that put on this seminar, and Chief Impact Officer Cullen White went on stage at the event and scolded the non-binary attendees. "Simply put, some of you lied when you registered. And as evidenced by the stacks and stacks of resumes you're passing out, you did so because you thought you could come here and take space to try and get a job," he said. Who the hell is he to question non-binary people? That's so non-binarist. Cannibalism. Chomp chomp.

4. THE SHOW YOUR ASS THEORY.

If you were to do the genealogy on this theory, you would find it is related to David Horowitz's "Anti-Anti-Communist Theory." If you've been listening to the podcast for a while, you're most likely very familiar with it. Early on, Dan used to get a lot of emails from people asking, "Dan, why is it that the media keeps doing extra Trump stories and making things up knowing that it's only helping him rise in the polls?" Dan would tell them, "This is the media showing their ass," and they would ask, "What the heck is that?" Just like everything the media does when it comes to Donald Trump and Republicans, they have to find the most childish way to insult them, and when one member does it, the next one has to go one better. By childish, I mean they want to show their butts like they're mooning you. It's been a historical insult. So why would the media do that? Why would they embarrass themselves and essentially moon America and make up stupid things like the Russia collusion stuff and quid pro quo impeachment stuff knowing that it's false, and they're going to be made to look stupid? They're mooning America. Why would they do that? The answer is related to the Anti-Anti-Communist Theory. That theory holds that we are anti-communist. So, anything that has its roots in communism or communist theory, we are against. Those who hate us may or may not hate communism, but their hate for us outweighs that, so if it's communist or not, it doesn't matter; they are just against whatever we're for or for what we're against. This relates to the fact that the media, because they really believed Trump was a "fascist Nazi," wanted to show their colleagues how much they reviled Donald Trump. So, they gave up any journalistic ethics, and they had to one-up each other on the craziness. As Dan said, "They would one-up each other. So, one media person would say, 'I think Trump rigged the election.' Another one would say, 'I think he rigged it with his entire team,' and then another would say, 'I think he rigged it with the Russians.' Then another goes, 'I think they rigged it with the Russians, and I think there's a pee pee tape.' Then yet another does a hold my beer thing and says, 'There's a pee pee tape, and Michael Cohen tried to get it in Prague!' Not any of this was based in any reality at all. But because they all had to show America their butts and humiliate themselves, now you can understand why. It's the anti-anti-communist thing in disguise. They just needed again to rebel against something. So, whatever you are for, they are against. So whatever Trump was for, they're against, and whatever Trump's against, they are for." For example, if Trump were to come out tomorrow and give this long-winded speech against white supremacists like he did after the Charlottesville thing (for the eleven billionth time, he condemned white supremacists and neo-Nazis; you can read the transcript, media; it happened), it wouldn't be surprising if the media was like, you know, they're not so bad. Because they're that crazy. They're legit that crazy.

5. THE VINNY/BROCK LESNAR THEORY.

Dan grew up with a guy named Vinny. Vinny was not a big guy and he didn't know how to fight. But Vinny would never back down from anybody and would fight everybody who wanted to, even when there was no way he was going to win. A lot of potential opponents would back down because they were afraid Vinny was crazy. This prevented a lot of other altercations he may have gotten into. Brock Lesnar is one of the biggest baddest MMA fighters of all time. If you had a problem with Brock Lesnar, you're not going to even entertain the thought of wanting to fight him, so no one wants to start anything with him. How does this apply to politics? It's definitely a leadership style with our politicians. The Soviet Union saw Ronald Reagan as a Brock Lesnar type, so even though the American media was worried Reagan would get us into nuclear war, the Soviets knew he was not to be messed with. Donald Trump is more like Vinny. The Russians would threaten certain actions, and Trump would respond with things like, "I'll bomb Moscow." The Russians didn't know whether to take him seriously or not because they thought he just might be crazy enough to do it. This is why they didn't invade Ukraine while he was President. Joe Biden is neither. This is why he is the most dangerous President we've had. Our adversaries neither fear nor respect him, which is what makes him a danger to us.

CHAPTER 10

LAGNIAPPE

Lagniappe is a word you'll hear mainly in South Louisiana, and it means giving a little something extra. As I went into great detail on a lot of P1 material in this book, there are a few other little things that are often referenced that qualify under the "if you know, you know" rule. So here we go in no specific order:

- The Dark Web Series. These are just parodies that my strange little brain comes up with from time to time. The first time I ever allegedly attempted a "dark web" segment, I had overheard Dan talking with Gui about Jen Psaki and the absolute hilariousness of her alleged handling of Peter Doocy being referred to as "Psaki bombs." Dan mentioned to Gui that we needed to come up with a term closer to reality, and after thinking about it for a second, I said, "We should call it a Psaki bong, because you have to be high to

117

believe anything she says." He loved it. So the next day, I had a fake commercial ready to go for the Psaki Bong. I had no idea how Dan was going to use this, so he came up with this idea that I searched all around the dark web, risking all kinds of viruses and malware to infect the network computer systems to find these products. The audience responded positively, so anytime an idea struck, I would go to work. I think the next one I did was "The Dumb Speaker," which instead of asking Alexa what the weather is, for example, you would ask Alexandria, as in AOC. And of course her answer would be, "The world is gonna end in twelve years if we don't address climate change." There have been series that have been developed too, like *Things That Never Happened* that highlights the many stories Joe Biden tells that have been completely debunked or easily disproven and *Whisky Tango Foxtrot Is She Saying* that highlights all the incredible insight from Kamala Harris. The one we got the most response to was when Joe Biden was caught mumbling at the United Nations, and Dan was trying to interpret what he was saying, and the best we could figure was him saying, "The Maria Giavolo Institution," so I put together an ad for the institute, and the rest is history.

- 8. The Bongino Rule. Not to be confused with Bongino's Golden Rules, this is a stand-alone and applies only to news cycles. The rule, simply stated, is whenever a news story breaks, wait forty-eight to seventy-two hours before commenting on it. The purpose of this is to have all the information you can and see how the story changes, which it most definitely will, before giving your opinions on the matter. So many times, those on cable news will throw out speculations that always turn out to be incorrect because they are just reporting whatever they hear, and then later have to go back and retract. You won't get that on this show. It's always better to be right than first.

- During Commercial Breaks. While you're hearing commercials, there is silence on our end. Since Dan is in Florida, and I'm in Texas, we want to make sure we haven't lost connection and avoid another goofy glue incident. Typically, I play music down the line so he knows we're still connected. When we started, I had no idea what kind of music he liked, so I asked for a few suggestions, and as we got to know each other better, I knew what to play. We started with '90s pop rock favorites like Nirvana, some classic rock like Pink Floyd, but now it's mostly country. We'll have different country artists that Dan likes, like Lainey Wilson, Jo Dee

Messina, Ashley Cooke, and every Friday, it's Morgan Wallen Friday.

- Dopey Media Talking Head Olympics. This is the medal stand for the top three biggest morons in the media. Brian Stelter had the gold medal for a long time, but he actually lost out to Joy Reid, which, rumor has it, this is the actual reason Brian was let go from CNN. To let someone from a competing network out-dumb you is unforgivable to CNN, so obviously Stelter had to go. Others who have been somewhere on the medal stand at one time or another are Chuck Todd and Don Lemon. Jim Acosta, Nicole Wallace, and Joe Scarborough always seem to be in the race as well.

- Roger Skaer Informational Video. Roger Skaer is an Instagram sensation who had the absolute greatest viral video of 2023. It's him explaining a simple graph describing how much you can find out in proportion to the amount you fuck around. It is simple, to the point, and something everyone in the country should see at least once and probably bookmark in case they have to refer to it later as a refresher. The single most important video you will ever see.

- College Football Mondays. Both Dan and I are big college football fans. As we were coming out of the COVID lockdowns, and teams were playing in front of actual crowds again, videos started popping up on social media of the crowds singing traditional songs. It was inspiring to see life look normal again. That's when we found out about a lot of these traditions. We thought it would be a good idea every Monday during the college football season to bump back into programming using one of the songs representing one of those schools as an homage to them.

- Our Correspondent Tiffany Gomas. Tiffany is the famous "lizard person on a plane" lady. Dan has made her our official correspondent on the scene everywhere to constantly point out that, "that motherf***er back there is not real." We thank her for her dedication to the cause. Fact checkers!! She's not really our official correspondent, or our correspondent at all, but we like to have fun with that drop when referring to things liberals say because what they usually say is not real.

- The Relaxium Lady. You've seen the Relaxium commercials constantly on Fox News. One stars a lovely woman named Rachel, and her delivery of the phrase, "I'm telling you..." just struck Dan, and now whenever Dan is telling you something, Rachel will always be there to emphasize his point.

- *Sir.* In an October 2020 interview on *60 Minutes* with President Donald Trump, he brought up the information about Hunter Biden's laptop. *60 Minutes* used to be the premier investigative journalism television show. Like the rest of the mainstream media, now they are just state propagandists, and in this particular interview, the hapless Leslie Stahl, who had done no research on the laptop, insisted on telling President Trump that there was no proof of anything on that laptop or that the laptop was even real. In one exchange when the president is trying to inform her about it, Leslie says, "Sir..." in this frustrated tone and unwittingly made *60 Minutes* into the *Sir* show on *The Dan Bongino Show*.

- The FCC Ruling on Cursing. It's to the point now where Dan doesn't even ask a full question anymore. If you ever hear him stop and ask, "Jim, the FCC? Any word? Still no?" this is exactly what we're talking about. The FCC will not let him curse on the radio, but should he, which has happened three times so far, I have the trusty dump button.

- Muttleys. These are exclusive to the podcast. Muttley was a character in the Hanna-Barbera cartoon *Wacky Races* and had a distinctive laugh. This is the drop Joe uses at appropriate times to accentuate a certain point of ridiculousness that Dan is making. The number of Muttleys determines how stupid the issue in question is. It's an algebraic equation that only Joe knows that determines that number, but if the number of Muttleys reaches four, then the reason for using them must be really mind-numbingly stupid.

- It's Friday. This is also podcast exclusive. Joe was just very joyous of it being Friday on one particular day heading into the weekend, and the audience responded enthusiastically to his enthusiasm, and it's been a staple ever since.

- Flag It. This applies to both the podcast and the radio show now. It started on the podcast, and Joe says he stole the idea from his traffic guy in Baltimore, Chuck Whitaker, who would hear something he liked for a commercial and would say, "Flag it!" That caught on with Dan, and now we will flag points or predictions we can now refer to when they come to pass.

CHAPTER 11

CLOSING TIME

We close out every week with the bumper "Closing Time" by Semisonic. Have that going through your head as we get to the end of this book. Just know this: We do this show for you. You are the most important part, the most important element in the success of this show. Without you, we have nothing. We do it to give you a sense of community, to give you a place you can come so you know that what you are already thinking, that things going on in your very lives are important, they are seen; we recognize what is going on, and we are right there with you to get you through these troubling times. We will do it passionately, sincerely, with the seriousness it deserves and the ridicule it deserves. Everything you get when you tune in to the podcast and the radio show is as real as it gets. There is nothing fake going on here. We will bare everything to you—no secrets, no lies, no agenda except pushing the absolute values that were given to us in our founding documents: that we have the God-given rights to life, liberty, and the pursuit of happiness, that all men are created equal, and for the purposes of these shows, and the lives of all Americans, that we have the right to free expression.

Benjamin Franklin famously replied when asked what kind of government the Constitutional Convention had given them, "A republic, if you can keep it." Ronald Reagan in his first inaugural address as governor of California said, "Freedom is a fragile thing and is never more than one generation away from extinction. It is not ours by way of inheritance; it must be fought for and defended constantly by each generation, for it comes only once to a people. And those in world history who have known freedom and then lost it have never known it again." May we all do our part in doing everything we can to make sure this generation is not the last to know a free nation.

ACKNOWLEDGMENTS

My family has always been the most important thing in my life. I want to thank my mom, Andrea, and my dad, Jerry, for raising me to love the country and do the right thing. My wife, Toni, for always supporting me and keeping me centered through all the good and all the hard times. My kids, Nicolas and Mia, for giving me the purpose to do whatever I had to do to make a good life for all of us. To all my St. Rose of Lima family, those were the best of times and couldn't have grown up around better people.

There are so many people in the radio industry who were instrumental to getting me where I am right now: Chuck Brinkman, Ken "Hubcap" Carter, Scott Reese and Kate Garvin at KLUV, Bill Pasha, Jim and Melissa Sharpe, and John McCarty at Star 105. Scott Savage, Rick Torcasso, Dan Pearman, Stubie Doak, Holly Stone, Johnny Stone, Toni Trueblood, Martha Martinez, Dave Cooley, and the great AW Pantoja for making Young Country one of the greatest experiences of my life. Bob McNeil for believing in AW and I for a talk radio shot that we had no business getting but thank God we did. Scott Masteller for first and second chances at ESPN. Leon McWhorter, Bryan Jester, Darren Silva, and Robin Jones Doak for bringing things out in me I wasn't sure I even had in me. Linda O'Brian who, even though we were competitors, always showed support and friendship. Bart Tessler, Kevin Delaney, Theresa Gage, and Robert Barowski for shepherding me through a seven-year gauntlet to come out clean on the other side and believing in me to take on this massive task of filling this legendary timeslot with one of the greatest talents I've ever worked with. James Golden for his kind words and his blessing. To our great guest hosts, Kira Davis, Lisa Boothe, Moon Griffon, Kurt Schlichter, Vince Coglianese, Jason Rantz, and Mary Walter, thanks for being our friends and helping us still sound great when Dan is out. And of course Dan Bongino, who didn't know me from Adam, and took a chance that I might know a thing or two about this. Thanks for an amazing ride.

I know I probably left out many I should mention here, but one I won't ever forget is my manager from my first job when I was sixteen at Godfather's Pizza, Ronda Mary. You weren't afraid to tell me I wasn't hacking it and straightened me out to recognize that working hard is the only way to approach anything, and stuck with me long enough for me to figure it all out.

ABOUT THE AUTHOR

Born and bred in Brooklyn, New York, and a Texan since 1981, Jim Verdi is a graduate of the University of Texas at Arlington in communications. Jim is a radio veteran of thirty-five years across many formats, with almost half of that in talk radio, and has worked in the DFW area his entire career. Married for thirty-plus years to a fantastic wife, Toni, with two adult children, Nicolas and Mia, and a dog dad to Nola and Marley, Jim is passionate about baseball, particularly the New York Mets. He loves history, particularly American history, and is an award-winning barbecue pitmaster and smoked meat aficionado.